Fruit of the Vine

Fruit of the Vine

A Biblical Spirituality of Wine

Mark G. Boyer

WIPF & STOCK · Eugene, Oregon

FRUIT OF THE VINE
A Biblical Spirituality of Wine

Copyright © 2017 Mark G. Boyer. All rights reserved. Except for brief quotations in critical publications or reviews, no part of this book may be reproduced in any manner without prior written permission from the publisher. Write: Permissions, Wipf and Stock Publishers, 199 W. 8th Ave., Suite 3, Eugene, OR 97401.

Wipf & Stock
An Imprint of Wipf and Stock Publishers
199 W. 8th Ave., Suite 3
Eugene, OR 97401

www.wipfandstock.com

PAPERBACK ISBN: 978-1-5326-1752-2
HARDCOVER ISBN: 978-1-4982-4225-7
EBOOK ISBN: 978-1-4982-4224-0

Manufactured in the U.S.A.   MARCH 30, 2017

Dedicated to the Moreheads:
Kristopher and Janet

In vino veritas.

Contents

Abbreviations | *ix*
Introduction | *xiii*

1 **Biblical Vineyard Stories** | 1
    Song of the Vineyard
    Joseph and the Cup-
        bearer's Dream
    Jotham's Fable
    Naboth's Vineyard
    Restoration
    Parable of the Tenants
    Matthean Allegory
        (Parable): Laborers
    Matthean Allegory
        (Parable): Two Sons
    Fruit of the Vine
    Jesus the Vine
    Turning Water into Wine
    Conclusion

2 **Picking Grapes** | 30
    Eating from One's Own
        Vine
    Dressing Vines
    Ripe Grapes
    Clusters of Grapes
    Grape-Gatherer

3 **Processing Grapes** | 35
    Treading Grapes
    Wine Press

4 **Types of Wine** | 38
    Sweet Wine
    Sour Wine
    Common Wine
    New Wine
    Wine Mixed with Water
    Wine Mixed with Myrrh

5 **Storage of Wine** | 44
    Vat
    Skins
    Wine Jar
    Vessel
    Storehouses for Wine

CONTENTS

6 **Measuring and Tasting Wine | 50**
    A Bath
    A Measure
    Tasting Wine

7 **Wine with Food | 54**
    Bread and Wine
    Eating and Drinking

8 **Effects of Wine | 57**
    Gladness
    Cheer
    Bitterness
    Drunkenness
    Merriment

9 **No Wine-Drinking | 62**
    Nazirites
    Ministry
    Rechabites

10 **Offering | 66**
    Drink Offering 1
    Drink Offering 2
    First Fruits
    Support of Ministers

11 **Metaphor for Life | 71**
    Wine Is Life
    Wine Is a Banquet
    Wine Is Love
    Wine Is a Woman
    Wine Is a Friend

12 **Metaphor for Abundance | 76**
    Full Yield
    Wealth
    Blessing
    Future Blessings
    Not Gathering All Grapes

13 **Metaphor for Poverty | 81**
    Lack of Wealth
    Destroyed
    Withered
    Sour Grapes
    Devoured

14 **Metaphor for Wrath | 86**
    Wine Press 1
    Wine Press 2
    Cup of Wrath
    No Wine-Drinking

15 **Metaphor for Blood | 91**
    Blood of the Grape
    Blood of the (New) Covenant
    Thanksgiving
    Drink Offering
    Fruit of the Vine

Other Books by Mark G. Boyer | 97
Bibliography | 99

Abbreviations

CB (NT) = Christian Bible (New Testament)

Acts	Acts of the Apostles
1 Cor	First Letter of Paul to the Corinthians
Eph	Letter of Paul to the Ephesians
John	John's Gospel
Luke	Luke's Gospel
Mark	Mark's Gospel
Matt	Matthew's Gospel
Rev	Revelation
Rom	Letter of Paul to the Romans
1 Tim	First Letter of Paul to Timothy
Titus	Letter of Paul to Titus

HB (OT) = Hebrew Bible (Old Testament)

Amos	Amos
1 Chr	First Book of Chronicles
2 Chr	Second Book of Chronicles
Dan	Daniel
Deut	Deuteronomy
Eccl	Ecclesiastes
Esth	Esther
Exod	Exodus

Ezek	Ezekiel
Ezra	Ezra
Gen	Genesis
Hag	Haggai
Hos	Hosea
Isa	Isaiah
Jer	Jeremiah
Job	Job
Joel	Joel
Judg	Judges
1 Kgs	First Book of Kings
2 Kgs	Second Book of Kings
Lam	Lamentations
Lev	Leviticus
Mal	Malachi
Mic	Micah
Neh	Nehemiah
Num	Numbers
Obad	Obadiah
Prov	Proverbs
Ps	Psalm
Pss	Psalms
1 Sam	First Book of Samuel
2 Sam	Second Book of Samuel
Song	Song of Songs (Song of Solomon)
Zech	Zechariah
Zeph	Zephaniah

OT (A) = Old Testament (Apocrypha)

Add Esth	Additional Chapters in Esther (Greek Version)
Bel	Bell and the Dragon (Daniel)
Jdt	Judith
2 Macc	Second Book of Maccabees
Sir	Sirach (Ecclesiasticus)
Tob	Book of Tobit
Wis	Wisdom (of Solomon)

Abbreviations

Notes on the Bible

The Bible is divided into two parts: The Hebrew Bible (Old Testament) and the Christian Bible (New Testament). The Hebrew Bible consists of thirty-nine named books accepted by Jews and Protestants as Holy Scripture. The Old Testament also contains those thirty-nine books plus seven to fifteen more named books or parts of books called the Apocrypha or the Deuterocanonical Books; the Old Testament is accepted by Catholics and several other Christian denominations as Holy Scripture. The Christian Bible, consisting of twenty-seven named books, is also called the New Testament; it is accepted by Christians as Holy Scripture. Thus, in this work:

—Hebrew Bible (Old Testament), abbreviated HB (OT), indicates that a book is found both in the Hebrew Bible and the Old Testament;

—Old Testament (Apocrypha), abbreviated OT (A), indicates that a book is found only in the Old Testament Apocrypha and not in the Hebrew Bible;

—and Christian Bible (New Testament), abbreviated CB (NT), indicates that a book is found only in the Christian Bible or New Testament.

In notating biblical texts, the first number refers to the chapter in the book, and the second number refers to the verse within the chapter. Thus, HB (OT) Isa 7:11 means that the quotation comes from Isaiah, chapter 7, verse 11. OT (A) Sirach 39:30 means that the quotation comes from Sirach, chapter 39, verse 30. CB (NT) Mark 6:2 means that the quotation comes from Mark's Gospel, chapter 6, verse 2.

In the HB (OT) and the OT (A), the reader often sees LORD (note all capital letters). Because God's name (Yahweh or YHWH, referred to as the Tetragrammaton) is not to be pronounced, the name Adonai (meaning *Lord*) is substituted for Yahweh when a biblical text is read. When a biblical text is translated and printed, LORD (cf. Gen 2:4) is used to alert the reader to what the text actually states: Yahweh. Because some scholars referenced in this book use Yahweh or YHWH, the author has maintained their usage but presented LORD in parentheses after the divine name. Furthermore, when the biblical author writes Lord Yahweh, printers present Lord GOD (note all capital letters for GOD; cf. Gen 15:2) to avoid the printed ambiguity of LORD LORD. When the reference is to Jesus, the word printed is Lord (note capital L and lower case letters; cf. Luke 11:1). When writing about a lord (note all lower case letters (cf. Matt 18:25) with servants, no capital L is used.

Introduction

The title of this book, *Fruit of the Vine: A Biblical Spirituality of Wine*, describes grapes grown in vineyards and processed into wine during the time biblical authors were writing their books. Using only biblical references, this book explores vineyard stories (preparing land, planting vines, digging a press, building a tower, etc.); picking and processing grapes; making, storing, measuring, tasting, and drinking wine; the effects of drinking wine; those who did not drink wine; the offering of wine; and wine as a metaphor for life, abundance, poverty, wrath, and blood. With almost five hundred biblical references to such aspects of vine-growing and wine-making, only a few can be explored here.

In fifteen chapters, there are seventy reflections, the goal of which is to develop a biblical spirituality of wine. Each chapter has two to six entries based on the chapter title, except for chapter 1 which has twelve entries. Each part of every chapter consists of five parts.

INTRODUCTION

1. The name of an aspect of vine-growing or wine-making indicates the focus of the chapter.

2. A few verses or sentences from a biblical text are provided. The text may be from the Hebrew Bible (Old Testament), the Old Testament (Apocrypha), or the Christian Bible (New Testament).

3. A reflection follows the text. The reflection presents some of the context for the text, attempting to surface its meaning. It also presents other references to the topic in other biblical sources. The short reflection is not to be understood as exhaustive; it is but a sampling, a sketch of the topic in biblical literature. It is designed to get the reader to stop and consider the wondrous works of God in wine.

4. The reflection is followed by a question for personal meditation and/or journaling. The question functions as a guide for personal appropriation of the message of the reflection, thus leading the reader into personal meditation and/or journaling and personal prayer. The meditation/journal question is designed to foster a process of actively applying the reflection to one's life. The question gets one started; where the meditation/journaling goes cannot be predetermined. It may be a single statement or an idea with which one lingers for a few minutes, a few hours, or a few days. The process has no end; the reader decides when he or she has finished exploring the topic because he or she needs to attend to other things.

5. A prayer concludes the exercise and summarizes the original theme announced in the title, which was explored in the reflection and which served as the foundation for the meditation/journaling.

The word *spirituality* is formed from the word *spirit*. It means the fact or condition of being spirit, and it refers to that aspect each person shares—that invisible nature some call soul, being, essence, breath, wind, etc. Since all people participate in the spirit that animates all—a universal spirit—a spirituality of wine is an attempt to connect the spirit in wine to the universal spirit all share in the hope of nourishing the individual's spirit. It is no accident that wine is broadly categorized as a spirit, that is, alcohol. It is also no accident that it is often referred to as a mystical beverage.

In the biblical world, wine was a staple drink. While drunkenness was not acceptable, drinking wine was, especially the several cups of red wine poured at Passover. It may be due to wine's appeal to all five senses. Its bouquet can be smelled; its complexity, often compared to fruit, can be tasted; its shades of red, designating its body, can be seen as it clings to or quickly runs down the inside of a glass. When a wine bottle is held in place with one hand while its cork is removed with another, one can hear the pop as the cork leaves the bottle's neck, feel the bottle and the cork, and smell the aromas emerging from the cork and the bottle. The gurgle of the wine leaving the bottle as it is poured into a glass adds to the auditory experience of enjoying a glass of wine.

The Greeks had a god of wine, Dionysus, and the Romans called him Bacchus. The dark red liquid he gave to people represented life (blood) and strength, love and friendship, and transformation. Wine is a major sign of transformation first in the ongoing process of growth, harvest, death. Second, wine-making is the result of breaking whole grapes into parts and integrating the parts into a whole—grapes into wine. The grapes themselves represent transformation from blossom, sunlight, and water. While the wine is aged, it undergoes even more transformation.

Sharing a bottle of wine represents further transformation. A few people come together and uncork this already, multiple-times-transformed beverage. Then, just as individual grapes are pressed to become one vat of juice, which through fermentation becomes wine, those who clink glasses together and share wine enter a deeper unity. They share spirit(s) with each other through the wine. That is why *in vino veritas*—in wine there is truth. A person drinking wine is very likely to speak truth in his or her thoughts, desires, and experiences that give meaning to life. The spirituality of each individual is enhanced by all the others who share spirit(s) engendered by the bottle of wine. Like a vat of grape juice that is

Introduction

transformed into wine, people are changed when they share spirit with each other through the medium of wine.

Using This Book

This book can be used at any time a person desires to develop further his or her spiritual life. It can be used in one's home as a daily exercise for several months, or the parts of each entry may be spread over several days or a week. This book can also be used during a retreat or on days set aside for reflection. Small groups of people might use it, reading its entries, sharing their reflections, and closing with its concluding prayer.

Shapiro encourages people to "talk about the sacred, the wondrous, and the awe-inspiring."[1] He urges people to "[s]hare with each other [their] respective sense of wonder and see if that doesn't open into different conversation about life, meaning, and purpose."[2] While he limits his remarks to reading the HB (OT), his words also hold true for reading the CB (NT); both are ways "to deepen [our] understanding of who [we are] and of what—for better and for worse-[we are] capable of,"[3] especially with a glass of wine in hand.

The book is designed to help the reader grow in spirituality through reflecting on wine. The vineyard and all it produces can reveal the divine if a person but opens his or her eyes to see. The Bible contains some of the truths that human ancestors have recorded about wine, and modern readers are enriched by what they have left. Indeed, the few footnotes that document ideas that this author has borrowed from others attest to that fact. The author hopes that these reflections will further the reader's spiritual journey and process for his or her descendants.

---

1. Shapiro, "Roadside Assistance," 19.
2. Ibid.
3. Ibid., 20.

1

Biblical Vineyard Stories

Song of the Vineyard

Scripture: "My beloved had a vineyard on a very fertile hill." (Isa 5:1b)

Reflection: The HB (OT) prophet Isaiah presents the epitome of vineyard stories. Bibles usually label Isaiah's tale as the song of the vineyard. It reveals what went into creating, maintaining, and harvesting a vineyard. "Let me sing for my beloved my love-song concerning his vineyard," begins Isaiah's story (Isa 5:1a).

> My beloved had a vineyard on a very fertile hill. He dug it and cleared it of stones, and planted it with choice vines; he built a watchtower in the midst of it, and hewed out a wine vat in it; he expected it to yield grapes, but it yielded wild grapes. And now, inhabitants of Jerusalem and people of Judah, judge between me and my vineyard. What more was there to do for my vineyard that I have

not done in it? When I expected it to yield grapes, why did it yield wild grapes? And I will tell you what I will do to my vineyard. I will remove its hedge, and it shall be devoured; I will break down its wall, and it shall be trampled down. I will make it a waste; it shall not be pruned or hoed, and it shall be overgrown with briers and thorns; I will also command the clouds that they rain no rain upon it. For the vineyard of the LORD of hosts is the house of Israel, and the people of Judah are his pleasant planting; he expected justice, and he saw bloodshed; righteousness, but heard a cry! (Isaiah 5:1b–7)

Literal Level: Roberts states that "the poem operates on several different levels and participates in several different genres. On the literal level, it is a song about a man's vineyard. . . . "[1] As the HB (OT) Book of Genesis states, "Noah, a man of the soil, was the first to plant a vineyard" (Gen 9:20).

Love Song: Roberts also states that vineyard "is a standard metaphor for one's 'beloved' in Israelite love poetry" and "the song was probably heard metaphorically as a love song . . . of unrequited love."[2] Nowhere is this more evident than in the HB (OT) erotic love poem known as the Song of Songs or Song of Solomon. Ryken states, "Fertile vines produced luscious grapes, pleasing to the taste and, when fermented, intoxicating. It is not surprising, considering the general use of agricultural images for sexuality, that the vine is frequently employed in [this] most sensual of all biblical poems. . . . "[3] Vineyard serves as a metaphor for a woman's body. The unnamed woman states that her brothers made her keeper of the vineyards, but her own vineyard she has not kept (Song 1:6), that is, she has not remained a virgin or chaste. She compares her beloved to precious aromatic scents which she puts between her breasts, that is, a cluster of henna blossoms in the vineyards (Song 1:14). She declares her beloved to be fruit sweet to her taste (Song

---

1. Roberts, *First Isaiah*, 71.
2. Ibid.
3. Ryken, *Dictionary*, 916.

2:3). He acknowledges that the vines are in blossom and give forth fragrance (Song 2:13), and he concludes, declaring: "Catch us the foxes, the little foxes, that ruin the vineyards—for our vineyards are in blossom" (Song 2:15). The little foxes in the song—a reference to the dangers of their lovemaking—also echo the story of Samson in the HB (OT) Book of Judges. Samson catches three hundred foxes, ties their tails together in pairs, places a lit torch between each pair of tails, and sets them loose to burn the vineyards of the Philistines (Judg 15:4-5), known as the vineyards of Timnah (Judg 14:5).

The vineyard serves as a setting for passionate lovemaking. The woman goes to the orchard to see whether the vines have budded (Song 6:11) and to meet the man. He, too, invites her to "go out early to the vineyards, and see whether the vines have budded, whether the grape blossoms have opened" for there he will give her his love (Song 7:12). He hopes that her breasts be like clusters of the vine (Song 7:7, 8b) and that her kisses be like the best wine that goes down smoothly, gliding over lips and teeth (Song 7:9). At the end of the poem the man declares that his vineyard, the woman, is better than Solomon's vineyard, whose fruit was worth much silver. His vineyard, his lover, belongs to him (Song 8:12). Similarly, Psalm 128, states that the wife of a man who fears the LORD will be like a fruitful vine within his house (Ps 128:3a).

Image of Israel: "Israel was a land of vineyards," states Ryken.[4] "... [I]t is not surprising that the vine and the vineyard, so characteristic of this country's agricultural fertility, serve as a potent image for the land itself."[5] Referring to the land of Judah, the prophet Ezekiel tells the princes of Judah in Babylonian captivity that their "mother was like a vine in a vineyard transplanted by the water, fruitful and full of branches from abundant water" (Ezek 19:10).

"The parable [song, allegory] of the vineyard ... describes Israel as God's vineyard," states Ryken.[6] The prophet Hosea states this unequivocally: "Israel is a luxuriant vine that yields its fruit"

---

4. Ibid., 914.
5. Ibid.
6. Ibid., 915.

(Hos 10:1). "It is God's not only because God loves it, but because he painstakingly prepared the land and planted it. He also carefully protected it. In this way the parable describes God's election of Israel as a nation (Deut 7:7–11) and his providential care of it."[7] The psalmist states this when he addresses God singing, "You brought a vine out of Egypt; you drove out the nations and planted it. You cleared the ground for it; it took deep root and filed the land. The mountains were covered with its shade, the mighty cedars with its branches; it sent out its branches to the sea and its shoots to the River" (Ps 80:8–11). Likewise, one of Ezekiel's allegories begins with a seed, representing Zedekiah, who was set up as king of Judah by Nebuchadnezzar of Babylon. The seed

> sprouted and became a vine spreading out, but low; its branches turned toward him, its roots remained where it stood. So it became a vine; it brought forth branches, put forth foliage. And see! This vine stretched out its roots toward him; it shot out its branches toward him, so that he might water it. From the bed where it was planted it was transplanted to good soil by abundant waters, so that it might produce branches and bear fruit and become a noble vine. (Ezek 17:6, 7b–8)

Isaiah's Friend: Roberts notes that "Isaiah sings his love song about his friend's vineyard on behalf of his friend."[8] He adds, "Isaiah sings his love song for his friend, trying to convince the audience by the extended vineyard metaphor that it was through no fault of his friend that his friend's beloved did not reciprocate his love."[9] He continues:

> Isaiah's friend chose a fertile spur of hill country as the location for his vineyard. He did the necessary work of preparing the ground by digging it up to rid it of weeds and by removing the large stones that would impede growth. He planted the prepared vineyard with choice

---

7. Ibid.
8. Roberts, *First Isaiah*, 71.
9. Ibid.

vine stock, built a tower within it to protect it from animal and human depredations, and hued out a wine vat in anticipation of the harvest. Then he waited for the well-tended vineyard to produce an abundance of grapes, but all it produced were sour, unripe, diseased berries.[10]

Suddenly in the prophet's love song "the friend himself speaks through Isaiah in the first person," states Roberts.[11] "Now, speaking as his friend, he invites [the audience] to judge between him and his 'vineyard.' Such judgment is still within the realm of a love song about unrequited love," states Roberts.[12] Isaiah's friend asks two rhetorical questions about what else could he do and was not his expectation reasonable. The same idea is expressed by God through the prophet Jeremiah: " . . . I planted you [, Israel,] as a choice vine, from the purest stock. How then did you turn degenerate and become a wild vine?" (Jer 2:21)

Destruction of the Vineyard: From this vineyard Isaiah's friend expected a good harvest. When he does not get it, according to Roberts, "He threatens to remove the hedge and wall around the vineyard so that the animals may graze and trample the unfruitful vineyard. He will no longer cultivate and prune the vineyard but will let it grow up in thorns and thistles like uncultivated wasteland. He will even command the clouds not to rain on it."[13] Isaiah records other judgments using the vineyard metaphor. The LORD tells the elders and princes of his people that they have devoured the vineyard (Isa 3:14b); that every place where there used to be a thousand vines will become briers and thorns (Isa 7:23).

> . . . [T]he vines of Sibmah, whose clusters once made drunk the lords of the nations; their shoots once spread abroad and crossed over the sea. Therefore I weep . . . for the vines of Sibmah; for the shout over your fruit harvest . . . has ceased. Joy and gladness are taken away from . . .

10. Ibid.
11. Ibid.
12. Ibid., 72.
13. Ibid.

the vineyards; no songs are sung, no shouts are raised; no treader treads out wine in the presses; the vintage shout is hushed. (Isa 16:8abd–9ac, 10)

According to Ryken, there is irony here: "The irony is that a place where one normally finds joy has become a place of weeping."[14] Later, in Isaiah the LORD declares, "If [the vineyard] gives me thorns and briers, I will march to battle against it. I will burn it up" (Isa 27:4).

The prophet Jeremiah employs the vineyard destruction metaphor. The LORD tells him, "Go up through [Israel's] vine-rows and destroy . . . ; strip away her branches, for they are not the LORD's" (Jer 5:10). God promises to bring a nation to destroy Israel, and it will eat up her vines (Jer 5:17b). Many of her leaders "have destroyed [God's] vineyard, they have trampled down [his] portion, they have made [his] pleasant portion a desolate wilderness" (Jer 12:10). Echoing Isaiah's words about the vines of Sibmah, Jeremiah weeps. "Your branches crossed over the sea . . . ; your summer fruits and your vintage the destroyer has fallen. Gladness and joy have been taken away from the fruitful land of Moab; I have stopped the wine from the wine presses; no one treads them with shouts of joy; the shouting is not the shout of joy" (Jer 48:32–33).

Ezekiel approaches the destruction-of-the-vineyard metaphor using a series of questions, which he portrays the LORD asking about his vine: "Will it prosper? Will he not pull up its roots, cause its fruit to rot and wither, its fresh sprouting leaves to fade? No strong arm of a mighty army will be needed to pull it from its roots. When it is transplanted, will it thrive? When the east wind strikes it, will it not utterly wither, wither on the bed where it grew?" (Ezek 17:9–10) The psalmist echoes Ezekiel, when he sings to God asking, "Why then have you broken down [the vineyard's] walls, so that all pass along the way pluck its fruit? The boar from the forest ravages it, and all that move in the field feed on it" (Ps 80:12–13).

---

14. Ryken, *Dictionary*, 916.

Biblical Vineyard Stories

The prophet Hosea portrays God bluntly declaring, "I will lay waste [Israel's] vines. . . . I will make them a forest, and the wild animals shall devour them" (Hos 2:12ac). Joel describes how the wine-drinkers should wail and weep because the plague of locusts has lain waste the vines (Joel 1:7). Amos pronounces judgment on Samaria portraying the LORD declaring that he lay waste her vineyards (Amos 4:9); in all the vineyards there will be wailing (Amos 5:17). Recounting the plagues visited upon Egypt, the psalmist employs the destruction-of-the-vineyard metaphor as a judgment on Egypt: The Holy one of Israel destroyed their vines with hail (Pss 78:47; 105:33) but there is no such specific reference to this in the Book of Exodus.

House of Israel and Judah: Keeping in mind that Isaiah's song of the vineyard is about a man's vineyard and can be considered a love song, Roberts states that the "deepest level of meaning" is that "Yahweh [the LORD] is the friend, and the vineyard is the house of Israel and the men of Judah. . . . Thus, the love song is not just an ordinary love song, . . . but a theological love song and judicial parable rolled into one. . . . Yahweh looked for justice only to see bloodshed, for righteousness only to hear the cry of the oppressed."[15]

Meditation/Journal: What do you think is the modern equivalent of the vineyard love song? Explain.

Prayer: Beloved God, once you created a vineyard out of your people Israel, planting them like a vine in fertile soil, but they produced only wild grapes. After the vineyard was destroyed, you replanted it in the hope of a fruitful yield. Make of me a fruitful vine that I may bring forth abundant wine of good works in this life with the hope of sharing in your heavenly vineyard. Amen.

---

15. Roberts, *First Isaiah*, 72.

Joseph and the Cupbearer's Dream

Scripture: " . . . [T]he chief cupbearer told his dream to Joseph, and said to him, 'In my dream there was a vine before me, and on the vine there were three branches. As soon as it budded, its blossoms came out and the clusters ripened into grapes. Pharaoh's cup was in my hand; and I took the grapes and pressed them into Pharaoh's cup, and placed the cup in Pharaoh's hand.' Then Joseph said to him, 'This is its interpretation: the three branches are three days; within three days Pharaoh will lift up your head and restore you to your office; and you shall place Pharaoh's cup in his hand, just as you used to do when you were his cupbearer.'" (Gen 40:9–13)

Reflection: The vine plays a role in one of the stories associated with Jacob's son, Joseph, who was sold into Egyptian slavery but rose through the ranks ultimately to be second in command to Pharaoh. While Joseph is serving as second in command to the chief jailer, he has the opportunity both to hear and interpret the chief cupbearer's dream. Three days after Joseph hears the dream and interprets it for the cupbearer, on Pharaoh's birthday, he restores the cup bearer to his previous position (Gen 40:20–23). In this story, the vine represents restoration or renewal. The number three indicates that God is present in the cupbearer's dream and directing the future of Joseph.

Meditation/Journal: What recent dream do you remember that in some way predicted your future? Explain.

Prayer: You gave your servant, Joseph, the gift of dream-interpretation, LORD God, that he might be the instrument of salvation for your people. Help me to hear your voice in my dreams that I may serve you all the days of my life. All praise be to you now and forever. Amen.

Jotham's Fable

Scripture: "The trees once went out to anoint a king over themselves. . . . [T]he trees said to the vine, 'You come and reign over us.' But the vine said to them, 'Shall I stop producing my wine that cheers gods and mortals, and go to sway over the trees?'" (Judg 9:8, 12–13)

Reflection: The vine plays a role in Jotham's fable about the trees, which is itself an expression of cynicism about kings. All the useful trees refuse kingship because it will waste their abilities. For example, when the trees decide to anoint a king to rule over them, they tell the vine to come and reign over them, but the vine reminds them that it will have to stop producing wine that cheers gods and mortals to do so. Ultimately, the worthless bramble agrees to be king of the trees. That statement alone explains what the author of the Book of Judges thinks about kings! In this fable, the vine represents the pleasure it gives through wine.

Meditation/Journal: What pleasure does drinking wine give you? Explain.

Prayer: Through parables and fables, LORD, you teach your people to be grateful that you are their king, who provides the pleasure of drinking wine. Grant me moderation in enjoying the good cheer that you give now and forever. Amen.

Naboth's Vineyard

Scripture: " . . . Ahab said to Naboth, 'Give me your vineyard, so that I may have it for a vegetable garden, because it is near my house; I will give you a better vineyard for it; if it seems good to you, I will give you its value in money.' But Naboth said to Ahab, 'The LORD forbid that I should give you my ancestral inheritance.'" (1 Kgs 21:2–3)

Reflection: The First Book of Kings contains the story about "Naboth the Jezreelite" who "had a vineyard in Jezreel, beside the palace of King Ahab of Samaria" (1 Kgs 21:1). The story continues in this way: "Ahab went home resentful and sullen because of what Naboth the Jezreelite had said to him; for he had said, 'I will not give you my ancestral inheritance.' He lay down on his bed, turned away his face, and would not eat. His wife Jezebel came to him and said, 'Why are you so depressed that you will not eat?'" (1 Kgs 21:4) Ahab explained to her what had happened to him in his dealing with Naboth. "His wife Jezebel said to him, 'Do you now govern Israel? Get up, eat some food, and be cheerful; I will give you the vineyard of Naboth the Jezreelite'" (2 Kgs 21:7).

> So she wrote letters in Ahab's name and sealed them with his seal; she sent the letters to the elders and the nobles who lived with Naboth in his city. She wrote in the letters, "Proclaim a fast and seat Naboth at the head of the assembly; seat two scoundrels opposite him, and have them bring a charge against him, saying, 'You have cursed God and the king.' Then take him out, and stone him to death." The men of his city, the elders and the nobles who lived in his city, did as Jezebel had sent word to them. Then they sent to Jezebel, saying, "Naboth has been stoned; he is dead."
>
> As soon as Jezebel heard that Naboth had been stoned and was dead, Jezebel said to Ahab, "Go, take possession of the vineyard of Naboth the Jezreelite, which he refused to give you for money; for Naboth is not alive, but dead." As soon as Ahab heard that Naboth was dead, Ahab set out to go down to the vineyard of Naboth the Jezreelite, to take possession of it. (1 Kgs 21:8–11a, 14–16)

This story ends with the prophet Elijah meeting Ahab at the vineyard and accusing him of murder. Elijah tells him that his blood will be licked by dogs in the same place where Naboth was stoned. In this long account, the vineyard represents Naboth's ancestral inheritance, that is, a small portion of the land given by God to Abraham, Isaac, and Jacob and all their descendants. Ahab had no rights to the vineyard when Naboth refused to sell or trade it.

Meditation/Journal: Today, where do see the same injustice that was inflicted upon Naboth by Ahab?

Prayer: Gracious God, once you gave blessings and land to your chosen people, but some with power stole it from them. Open my eyes that I may see the injustices that surround me today. Give me the strength to speak against them that your justice may prevail now and forever. Amen.

Restoration

Scripture: "In days to come Jacob shall take root, Israel shall blossom and put forth shoots, and fill the whole world with fruit." (Isa 27:6)

Reflection: In the Bible, the vineyard metaphor is used by the major prophets as an image of restoration. Through Isaiah, God declares that on the day of the LORD Jacob will take root, Israel will blossom and put forth shoots, and fill the whole world with fruit. In other words, the destruction that ended the song of the vineyard in Isaiah 5:1–7 will be reversed. Likewise, when God creates new heavens and a new earth, people shall plant vineyards and eat their fruit (Isa 65:21). The prophet Jeremiah, too, portrays God declaring that his people "shall plant vineyards on the mountains of Samaria; the planters shall plant, and shall enjoy the fruit" (Jer 31:5); vineyards shall again be bought in the land (Jer 32:15). Likewise, the prophet Ezekiel declares that the Lord GOD's people shall plant vineyards (Ezek 28:26).

The minor prophets also use the vineyard to represent restoration. Once the LORD has lured his people back to the desert, he will give Israel her vineyards (Hos 2:15) and "they shall blossom like the vine, their fragrance shall be like the wine of Lebanon" (Hos 14:7b). The vine gives its full yield, states Joel (Joel 2:22). Amos is very clear: "I will restore the fortunes of my people Israel," declares the LORD, "and they shall plant vineyards and drink their wine" (Amos 9:14). In days to come states the prophet Micah, the people "shall all sit under their own vines" (Mic 4:4); they will be blessed with the yield of the vine (Hag 2:19). Zechariah writes, "On that day, says the LORD of hosts, you shall invite each other to come under your vine" (Zech 3:10) for "the vine shall yield its fruit" (Zech 8:12). In the prophet Malachi, God states that the vine in the field shall not be barren (Mal 3:11).

Meditation/Journal: What metaphor speaks of restoration for you today? Explain.

Prayer: In days to come, O LORD, you decree that Jacob will take root, that Israel will blossom and put forth shoots, and fill the whole world with fruit. Bring that day to fulfillment that I may share in the restoration you offer to your people now and forever. Amen.

Parable of the Tenants

Scripture: "[Jesus] began to speak to [the chief priests, the scribes, and the elders] in parables. 'A man planted a vineyard, put a fence around it, dug a pit for the wine press, and built a watchtower; then he leased it to tenants and went to another country." (Mark 12:1)

Reflection: In the CB (NT) there are only three major blocks of material that employ the vine and vineyard allegory. The first block builds on Isaiah's song of the vineyard. In the synoptic gospels of Mark, Matthew, and Luke, the material is known as the vineyard parable or the parable of the tenants. However, it is really an analogy. Originally written by the author of Mark's Gospel, it was copied and changed by both the author of Matthew's Gospel and the author of Luke's Gospel.

Beginning: In Mark's Gospel, the allegory begins with Jesus telling the parable to the chief priests, the scribes, and the elders. A man plants a vineyard, puts a fence around it, digs a pit for the wine press, and builds a watchtower; then he leases it to tenants and goes to another country. In Matthew's Gospel, this parable follows the analogy (parable) of a man having two sons, which will be treated below. Thus, Jesus continues to address the chief priests and the elders of the people (Matt 21:23), beginning, "Listen to another parable. There was a landowner who planted a vineyard, put a fence around it, dug a wine press in it, and built a watchtower. Then, he leased it to tenants and went to another country" (Matt 21:33). The opening line in Luke's Gospel indicates that Jesus is addressing only the people: "[Jesus] began to tell the people this parable: 'A man planted a vineyard, and leased it to tenants, and went to another country for a long time.'" (Luke 20:9). It is not difficult to see that Mark and Matthew (although slightly abbreviated) rely upon Isaiah 5:1b-2 for their beginning of the allegory. Luke shortens the introductory line dramatically.

First Slave(s): "When the season came, [the vineyard owner] sent a slave to the tenants to collect from them his share of the produce of the vineyard," states Mark's Gospel (Mark 12:2). "But they seized him, and beat him, and sent him away empty-handed" (Mark 12:3). Matthew rewrites those two verses from Mark, recording: "When the harvest time had come, [the vineyard owner] sent his slaves to the tenants to collect his produce. But the tenants seized his slaves and beat one, killed another, and stoned another" (Matt 21:34–35). Luke's shorter version of the narrative states: "When the season came, he sent a slave to the tenants to collect from them his share of the produce of the vineyard. But they seized him, and beat him, and sent him away empty-handed" (Luke 12:2–3). While Mark records the sending of a single slave, Matthew records the sending of at least three slaves (maybe even more), one of whom is beaten, one of whom is killed, and one of whom is stoned. As will be seen, the first slave that Luke records being sent will only be beaten and will be sent two more times.

Second Slave(s): Now according to Mark the vineyard owner "sent another slave to [the tenants]; this one they beat over the head and insulted" (Mark 12:4). According to Matthew, the owner "sent other slaves, more than the first; and [the tenants] treated them in the same way" (Matt 21:36). "Next he sent another slave; that one also they beat and insulted and sent away empty-handed," states Luke (Luke 20:11).

Third Slave(s): "Then [the vineyard owner] sent another [slave], and that one [the tenants] killed," states Mark. "And so it was with many others; some they beat, and others they killed" (Mark 12:4–5). Matthew does not record a third-sending of slaves, but Luke does: "And [the vineyard owner] sent still a third; this one also they wounded and threw out" (Luke 20:12).

Owner's Son Sent: Finally, the vineyard owner decides to send his son. Mark narrates: "He had still one other, a beloved son. Finally he sent him to them, saying, 'They will respect my son.' But those tenants said to one another, 'This is the heir; come, let us kill him, and the inheritance will be ours.' So they seized him, killed him, and threw him out of the vineyard" (Mark 12:6–8). Matthew shortens his Markan source, narrating: "Finally he sent his son to them, saying, 'They will respect my son.' But when the tenants saw the son, they said to themselves, 'This is the heir; come, let us kill him and get his inheritance.' So they seized him, threw him out of the vineyard, and killed him" (Matt 21:37–39). Luke adds to the inner dialogue of the vineyard owner, narrating: "Then the owner of the vineyard said, 'What shall I do? I will send my beloved son; perhaps they will respect him.' But when the tenants saw him, they discussed it among themselves and said, 'This is the heir; let us kill him so that the inheritance may be ours.' So they threw him out of the vineyard and killed him" (Luke 20:13–15a). In Mark's Gospel, the son is the fourth messenger to go to the vineyard. In Matthew's Gospel, the son is the third messenger to be sent to the tenants. Luke follows Mark and makes the son the fourth messenger. Into the vineyard owner's soliloquy about the tenants respecting his son, only Luke adds the hope that perhaps they will do so. In Mark, the tenants kill the son in the vineyard and then throw him out; in Matthew and Luke they throw him out and then kill him. The earliest versions of the allegory (parable) probably ended with the death of the son or the death of the tenants.

Application 1: The allegory differs in its conclusion just as it differs in is details. Mark's version asks rhetorically, "What then will the owner of the vineyard do?" and answers, "He will come and destroy the tenants and give the vineyard to others" (Mark 12:9). Matthew poses the question to the hearers, who reply with an answer: "'Now when the owner of the vineyard comes, what will he do to those tenants?' They said to him, 'He will put those wretches to a miserable death, and lease the vineyard to other tenants who will give him the produce at the harvest time'" (Matt 21:40–41). Luke follows Mark's rhetorical question-and-answer scenario: "What then will the owner of the vineyard do to them? He will come and destroy those tenants and give the vineyard to others" (Luke 20:15b–16a).

Before moving on to the second application of the allegory a few notes are necessary. According to Ryken, the vineyard theme in the HB (OT) has been changed by the authors of the CB (NT). "It is no longer ethnic Israel that is God's vineyard, but the kingdom of God."[16] He adds, "The landowner, who is surely meant to represent God, plants and protects a vineyard and then rents it to tenants who end up abusing his servants. The parable ends with a threat against those who misuse the vineyard."[17] Meier states that anyone even remotely familiar with Isaiah's song of the vineyard

> would easily recognize the vineyard as Israel, the owner of the vineyard as God, the servants sent by the owner as the prophets, and those who reject and kill the servants as the evil leaders of Israel (or more specifically, of Jerusalem). In addition, early Christian hearers of . . . the parable would immediately recognize the only son as Jesus, his violent death as his crucifixion, the punishment of the tenants as the destruction of Jerusalem, and the citation of . . . Psalm 118:22–23 as the announcement of Jesus' vindication by way of his resurrection [which will be examined shortly]. One would have to be totally ignorant of both Jewish and early Jewish-Christian traditions not to grasp most if not all of the allegory inherent

16. Ryken, *Dictionary*, 916–17.
17. Ibid., 917.

in and throughout the parable. Far from some adventitious contrivance, this allegory lies at the very core of the parable and in inextricably bound up with it.[18]

Application 2: As indicated in Meier's comments above, there is another application at the end of the allegory. In Mark's Gospel, Jesus asks: "'Have you not read this scripture: The stone that the builders rejected has become the cornerstone; this was the Lord's doing, and it is amazing in our eyes'"? When [the chief priests, the scribes, and the elders] realized that he had told this parable against them, they wanted to arrest him, but they feared the crowd. So they left him and went away" (Mark 12:10–12).

Matthew is much more direct in his application of the allegory. Matthew narrates:

> Jesus said to [the chief priests and the elders of the people], "Have you never read the scriptures: 'The stone that the builders rejected has become the cornerstone; that was the Lord's doing, and it is amazing in our eyes'? Therefore I tell you, the kingdom of God will be taken away from you and given to a people that produces the fruits of the kingdom. The one who falls on this stone will be broken to pieces; and it will crush anyone on whom it falls." When the chief priests and the Pharisees heard his parable, they realized that he was speaking about them. They wanted to arrest him, but they feared the crowds, because they regarded him as a prophet. (Matt 21:42–44)

Luke shortens the material he took from Mark, narrating:

> When [the chief priests and scribes with the elders] heard this, they said, "Heaven forbid!" But [Jesus] looked at them and said, "What then does this text mean: 'The stone that the builders rejected has become the cornerstone'? Everyone who falls on that stone will be broken to pieces; and it will crush anyone on whom it falls." When the scribes and chief priests realized that he had told this parable against them, they wanted to lay hands on him at that very hour, but they feared the people. (Luke 20:16b–19)

---

18. Meier, *Marginal Jew*, 86–7.

In both Mark and Matthew, Jesus quotes Psalm 118:22–23. In Luke, he only quotes Psalm 118:22. Because Matthew presents the Jewish leaders answering Jesus' question, they pronounce judgment on themselves. Matthew specifically states that the vineyard, that was a sign of the land and the Israelites, will be taken away from the Jewish leaders and given to a people, the church, composed of Jews and Gentiles, bearing fruit. Thus, the parable concludes with a threat against those who misuse the vineyard.

Thus, there are a number of meanings reassigned to the vineyard metaphor. First, in Mark's Gospel the vineyard allegory (parable) of the tenants serves as a prediction of the fall of Jerusalem. Since the author of Mark's Gospel most likely composed the allegory, he "has Jesus prophesying the destruction of Jerusalem, implicitly fitting the whole parable into the larger story of Jesus' ministry to his own people, his rejection by their leaders, and their subsequent punishment via the destruction of their ancient capital and temple" in 70 CE.[19] In Mark, the beloved son dies in the vineyard, and then he is thrown out. Thus, according to Mark, the reason Jerusalem fell to the Romans was because Jewish leadership failed to accept the authority of Jesus.

Given Matthew's strong anti-Jewish position, the author of this gospel places the allegory (parable) immediately after another one set in a vineyard, which will be examined below, clearly hinting that slaves represent the major and minor prophets in a line of three, the last being the son, Jesus. The first group of tenants represents the Jewish leadership, especially the Pharisees and to some degree the Sadducees in Matthew, who have rejected Jesus' teaching. The son's death, which takes place outside the vineyard, clearly echoes Jesus' death. Thus, for Matthew, the vineyard—now the kingdom of God—is given to a new group of tenants, namely, the Jews who believe in Jesus and the Gentiles, the components of Matthew's church.

The allegory (parable) of the vineyard in Luke's Gospel has been adjusted by the author to fit his own understanding. The Lukan Jesus tells the parable to the crowd, not to the chief priests, scribes, and elders who had just asked him about his authority to

19. Ibid., 123.

teach. In other words, Jesus turns away from them and tells the people listening to him about them. From a Lukan point of view this parable (allegory) is a very harsh condemnation of Jews in favor of Gentiles. Even the Jewish leadership is afraid of the people who believe in Jesus' teaching! Luke makes it clear that the beloved son is Jesus, who is taken out of the vineyard and killed. The shorter quotation from Psalm 118 serves as a summary-commentary about the death and resurrection of Jesus, indicating that the allegory (parable) in all three synoptic gospels is a post-Easter creation of the church. The stone worthless to a builder has become the cornerstone of a new vineyard filled with fruit-bearing Gentiles.

Both Matthew and Luke employ a saying from Q (meaning *Source*, and indicating a document used by both Matthew and Luke but unknown to Mark) about anyone falling on the rejected stone that has become the cornerstone will be broken, and that it will crush anyone upon whom it falls (Matt 21:44; Luke 20:18). This saying is probably an allusion to Daniel 2:34–35, 44–45, one of Daniel's dream interpretations about a stone destroying a statue, and Isaiah 8:14–15, a passage about the LORD being a stone one strikes against, a trap, and a snare for Jerusalem.

Meier accurately summarizes the three versions of the allegory (parable) stating:

> A Jewish-Palestinian audience of Jesus' time, listening to a well-known prophet and teacher as he addressed the religious leaders in the Jerusalem temple, could hardly miss the scriptural allusions, inherent in symbols like the vineyard, the owner of the vineyard sending his servants to make claims on those working in his vineyard, and the rejection of those servants by the workers. One would have to be ignorant not only of individual scriptural texts but also for the master narrative governing the Jewish Scriptures to miss the reference.[20]

---

20. Ibid.

Biblical Vineyard Stories

Meditation/Journal: How do you think Jesus would tell this parable (allegory) today? Be sure to think in terms of the vineyard owner, tenant farmers, slaves, and Jesus.

Prayer: LORD God, you planted a vineyard, put a fence around it, dug a pit for the wine press, and built a watchtower; then you leased it to tenants and went to another country. In the person of Jesus, your Son, Heavenly Father, you have opened the vineyard to all people willing to bear fruit. Grant that I may produce fruit in this life that leads to eternal life. I ask this in the name of Jesus Christ, who is Lord forever and ever. Amen.

Matthean Allegory (Parable): Laborers

Scripture: "The kingdom of heaven is like a landowner who went out early in the morning to hire laborers for his vineyard." (Matt 20:1)

Reflection: After having mentioned Matthew's anti-Jewish polemic in the allegory (parable) of the tenants (vineyard) above, it is good to look at two other allegories (parables) unique to Matthew's Gospel. Usually referred to as M or Special M to indicate that both allegories are found only in Matthew's Gospel and/or that the author of Matthew's Gospel wrote the allegories himself, these allegories feature a vineyard. Matthew 20:1-16 precedes the allegory of the tenants in the vineyard. The parable begins specifically connecting the vineyard to the kingdom of God, which Matthew prefers to call the kingdom of heaven. "The kingdom of heaven is like a landowner who went out early in the morning to hire laborers for his vineyard. After agreeing with the laborers for the usual daily wage, he sent them into the vineyard" (Matt 20:1-2). The analogy progresses with the vineyard owner hiring more laborers at nine o'clock, at noon, at three o'clock, and at five o'clock and sending them to work in his vineyard (Matt 20:3-7).

When evening comes, the vineyard owner tells his manager to pay the day laborers by beginning with the last who were hired and ending with the first who were hired. Thus, a reversal is occurring. So, when the manager first pays the day laborers hired last, those hired first expect to get more, but all receive the same daily wage. The first hired complain to the vineyard owner: "These last worked only one hour, and you have made them equal to us who had borne the burden of the day and the scorching heat" (Matt 20:12). The vineyard owner reminds them that he contracted with all the day laborers for the same daily wage (Matt 20:13).

If the reader understands the first day laborers as the Israelites (Jews) and the last as the Gentiles, with those in between being converts to Judaism, the parable is about God's (the vineyard owner's) graciousness towards all people. In other words, he invites all people—Jews and Gentiles—to work in his kingdom, no matter what time of the day they accept his invitation. Those Jews, maybe even Jewish-Christians, who are grumbling echo the various grumblings of the Hebrews, Israelites, and Jews throughout the HB (OT), too numerous to list here. This is why the parable ends with the vineyard owner, God, telling the grumbling laborers to take what they have earned and go. He is free to do whatever he pleases with what belongs to him (Matt 20:14–15a). He finishes by asking them: " . . . [A]re you envious because I am generous?" (Matt 20:15b) No answer is provided. Using the vineyard metaphor, which originally referred to the promised land and the Israelites, the Matthean Jesus has just moved back the metaphor's boundaries to the point that they encompass the whole world and its peoples and God's kingdom!

Appended to this allegory (parable) is one of the author's typical ways to end a story: "So the last will be first, and the first will be last" (Matt 20:16; cf. 19:30). While the day laborers hired last are the first to be paid, that is about the only application of the last line of the allegory. However, with the added context of Matthew's anti-Jewish polemic, it can refer to the Gentiles (the last) getting ahead of the Jews (the first) when it comes to the kingdom of heaven.

Meditation/Journal: At what time of the day did you begin work in the vineyard? How do you feel about everyone getting the same daily wage?

Prayer: Heavenly Father, in your kingdom justice is exactly the opposite of what it is on earth. You treat all the workers with mercy, no matter when they enter the kingdom. Bestow that same mercy upon me now and forever. Amen.

Matthean Allegory (Parable): Two Sons

Scripture: "What do you think? A man had two sons; he went to the first and said, 'Son, go and work in the vineyard today.' He answered, 'I will not'; but later he changed his mind and went." (Matt 21:28–29)

Reflection: The other unique Matthean allegory featuring a vineyard immediately precedes the allegory (parable) of the tenants in the vineyard. Thus, even before examining it, it is safe to say that the author of Matthew's Gospel sees some connection between the two stories. The allegory of the two sons emphasizes the importance of deeds or works while denigrating empty promises. However, it is set in a vineyard, which indicates that it also has something to say about the expansion of the understanding of Isaiah's song of the vineyard.

The Matthean Jesus begins by posing a question to the chief priests and the elders of the people, who had just questioned his authority to teach. He says:

> What do you think? A man had two sons; he went to the first and said, "Son, go and work in the vineyard today." He answered, "I will not"; but later he changed his mind and went. The father went to the second and said the same; and he answered, "I go, sir"; but he did not go. Which of the two did the will of the father? They said, "The first." (Matt 21:28–31b)

The man with two sons is a familiar story to Jewish ears. However, in this unique narrative, the first son represents the Gentiles, who at first said no to God, according to the popular Jewish perspective of the time, while the second son represents the Jews, who in Matthew's Gospel refuse to believe that Jesus is the Messiah. Again, attention must be given to the place of work: a vineyard. In Matthew's Gospel, the vineyard is one of the metaphors for the kingdom of heaven (God). Gentiles (the first son), who had at first not believed that Jesus is the Messiah, are entering Matthew's church, while Jews (the second son), who had been the recipient of Jesus' ministry, did not believe. So, when the Jewish leaders are asked to name which son did the will of the father, they end up indicting themselves with their answer; they declare that Gentiles are doing God's will!

The Matthean Jesus adds an explanation to the correct answer given by the Jewish leaders. "Jesus said to them, 'Truly I tell you, the tax collectors and the prostitutes are going into the kingdom of God ahead of you. For John came to you in the way of righteousness and you did not believe him, but the tax collectors and the prostitutes believed him and even after you saw it, you did not change your minds and believe him'" (Matt 21:31c-32). In other words, Jewish leaders heard the teaching of John the Baptist, but they rejected it, like the second son. However, the outcasts, the dirt of society, the tax collectors and prostitutes, accepted it, like the first son. Those who had placed themselves outside the acceptable standards of righteousness are declared by Jesus to be the righteous, and those who thought of themselves as righteous are declared to be unrighteous. Tax collectors were Jews who worked for the Roman occupation forces of Palestine; they made their living by raising the amount of the set Roman tax and pocketing the difference. They were considered apostates. Prostitutes are those who have received money for sexual intercourse or other sexual acts; they are considered unclean because of their contact with blood and semen. There are new residents in the vineyard, and the original ones are not pleased to have the new ones there!

Meditation/Journal: Who are the new residents in the vineyard (your city, neighborhood, street)? Are you pleased that they are there? If so, why? If not, why not?

Prayer: You have sent all people to go and work in your vineyard, almighty Father. Some have refused and later changed their mind; some have said yes, but never went. Grant me the grace always to do your will now and forever. Amen.

Fruit of the Vine

Scripture: Jesus said to his apostles, "... I tell you that from now on I will not drink of the fruit of the vine until the kingdom of God comes." (Luke 22:18)

Reflection: The second major block of vineyard material in the CB (NT) is a saying of Jesus found in Mark, Matthew, and Luke. In Mark's Gospel at the end of the Passover meal Jesus declares, "Truly I tell you, I will never again drink of the fruit of the vine until the day when I drink it new in the kingdom of God" (Mark 14:25). Matthew's version of the saying is this: "I tell you, I will never again drink of this fruit of the vine until the day when I drink it new with you in my Father's kingdom" (Matt 26:29). And Luke's version portrays Jesus stating, "... I tell you that from now on I will not drink of the fruit of the vine until the kingdom of God comes" (Luke 22:18). It is important to note that in Luke's Gospel, Jesus blesses the cup two times; this saying is attached to the first blessing of the cup. In Mark and Matthew there is only one cup blessing, and so the saying is attached to it.

In all accounts of the saying, vineyard serves as the background by labeling the wine the fruit of the vine. The vineyard represents a heavenly or messianic place of joy, much like the restorative descriptions found in the HB (OT) material above, especially the prophet Isaiah. While it is true to state that the saying reflects future joy in God's kingdom in Mark and Luke, for Matthew it is a turning point in salvation history; according to

Matthew's allegories (parables), the kingdom has been given to others. Minimally, the kingdom is open to others. The only residents of the vineyard are no longer Jews.

Meditation/Journal: Whom do you consider in the kingdom? What are your criteria for inclusion?

Prayer: Almighty God, your Son, Jesus, declared that he would never again drink of the fruit of the vine until the day when he drank it new in your kingdom. Bring your kingdom to fulfillment that I may join my Lord Jesus Christ in drinking the fruit of the vine forever and ever. Amen.

Jesus the Vine

Scripture: Jesus said, "I am the true vine, and my Father is the vinegrower." (John 15:1)

Reflection: The third major block of biblical material concerning the vine and the vineyard in the CB (NT) is found in John's Gospel. The Johannine Jesus tells his disciples:

> I am the true vine, and my Father is the vinegrower. He removes every branch in me that bears no fruit. Every branch that bears fruit he prunes to make it bear more fruit. You have already been cleansed by the word that I have spoken to you. Abide in me as I abide in you. Just as the branch cannot bear fruit by itself unless it abides in the vine, neither can you unless you abide in me. I am the vine, you are the branches. Those who abide in me and I in them bear much fruit, because apart from me you can do nothing. Whoever does not abide in me is thrown away like a branch and withers; such branches are gathered, thrown into the fire, and burned. My Father is glorified by this, that you bear much fruit and become my disciples. (John 15:1-6, 8)

It is not difficult to see that Jesus, not Israel, is now the true vine in the vineyard. The author of this discourse understood and employed the language of viticulture. The image is that of a vineyard, owned by God the Father, with a single, woody, tree-like vine growing in it. That vine is Jesus. From the vine grow branches that bear fruit. In order that the branches keep bearing fruit, they have to be pruned, cut back, cleansed, and the Father does this through Jesus' spoken (and written) word to his disciples. In order for the branches to remain alive, they cannot be cut from the vine. The Johannine language refers to this as *abiding in*. The vine is the source of life for the branches; the vine enables the branches to produce fruit. If the branch does not stay on the vine, it is thrown into a pile and burned. The goal of staying on the vine is great fruit production, which glorifies the Father and indicates that the branch is a disciple of Jesus.

After reminding the reader that metaphorically the vine is Israel in the HB (OT) and that "Israel is the vine as the peculiar object of the care of Yahweh, as the vine is the object of the care of its grower, and the plant from which he expects most fruit,"[21] McKenzie adds that "the vine is also a figure of luxuriant growth and of fertility."[22] Then, he discusses the Johannine replacement image of Jesus as the vine. "[I]t signifies the close union between Jesus and the disciples," states McKenzie. "The disciples derive their power to bear fruit only by a vital union with Jesus, a sharing of the same life which is the source of power and activity."[23]

Meditation/Journal: What fruit do you bear as a branch on the vine of Christ? How have you been pruned?

Prayer: Father, your Son, Jesus declared that he is the true vine, and you are the vinegrower who removes every branch in him that bears no fruit. Every branch that bears fruit you prune to make it bear more fruit. Keep me, a branch, connected to him, that abiding in him I may be much fruit now and into eternity. Amen.

---

21. McKenzie, *Dictionary*, 913.
22. Ibid.
23. Ibid.

Turning Water into Wine

Scripture: "On the third day there was a wedding in Cana of Galilee, and the mother of Jesus was there. Jesus and his disciples had also been invited to the wedding. When the wine gave out, the mother of Jesus said to him, 'They have no wine.'" (John 2:1–3)

Reflection: Vineyard stories would not be complete with spending time with the unique Johannine narrative of Jesus turning water into wine. The narrative begins on a third day. This detail immediately alerts the reader that something divine is going to occur here. And of course, wedding is one of those HB (OT) metaphors used often by the prophets to depict God's union with his people. The unnamed mother of Jesus makes only two appearances in John's Gospel: here and at the foot of the cross. These two appearances serve as a clue that there is some connection between this narrative and that of Jesus' death. One has to read all the material between these two bookends in order to discover the significance of the bookends.

Weddings often lasted for days. The bride and groom were responsible with the help of their families to serve food and drink to their guests who had come to celebrate with them. As fate would have it, the wine ran out. It is Jesus' mother who notifies him of this sad detail. He informs her that his hour has not yet arrived (John 2:4). Reading from one bookend to the other, one quickly discovers that the word *hour* refers to the suffering, death, and resurrection. But his mother is not sidetracked by his words; she orders the servants to do whatever he tells them. At this point in the story the dialogue stops and the narrator takes over: "Now standing there were six stone water jars for the Jewish rites of purification, each holding twenty or thirty gallons" (John 2:6). The astute reader will note that there are six stone water jars; six is an incomplete biblical number. To complete it, one more is needed, and it is found at the cross after Jesus' hour has arrived.

The Johannine Jesus tells the servants to fill the twenty-to-thirty gallon jars with water; that means that they minimally dumped one hundred twenty gallons of water into them or maximally one hundred eighty gallons! Jesus says no magic words; he does not wave his hand over the water; he does not even touch the water. He merely instructs the water-bearers to draw some and take it to the chief wine steward, who had no idea from where the wine had come. After tasting it he called the bridegroom aside and asked him why he saved the best wine for last. The usual custom was to serve the best wine first (John 2:9–10). The narrative ends with the narrator stating: "Jesus did this, the first of his signs, in Cana of Galilee, and revealed his glory, and his disciples believed in him" (John 2:11). The only other mention of this sign is in John 4:46 before Jesus does the second of his seven Johannine signs.

It is important to note that there is no bride in this story! Many people presume there to be one, but there is none mentioned. In Johannine story theology, the bride is the collective of people who see Jesus' signs and believe in him. That is the concept flowing between the two bookends of the wedding at Cana and Jesus' death on the cross. That is why Jesus announces that his hour has come (John 13:1); the later insertion of chapters 14–16 obscure this declaration so that it needs to be repeated again (17:1). That is why Jesus' mother makes her only other appearance at the cross (John 19:25), where the sixth jar of wine is found (John 19:29). That is why Jesus' final words in John, "It is finished" (John 19:30), refer back to the wedding that he began in chapter 2 of John's Gospel. The bride is collectively born from the side of Jesus as blood and water (John 19:34)—an unmistakable reference to wine and water, the Lord's Supper and Baptism—just like the first woman-wife was born from the side of the first man-husband (Gen 2:22–23). Thus, the wedding that began between Jesus, the groom, and collective believers, the bride, is complete with Jesus' death. Those who have seen his signs believe in him. The glory revealed at Cana is revealed again after Jesus' resurrection (John 20:8–9, 17, 19–20, 26–28) and led to the addition of another chapter to the book where more glory is revealed (John 21:7, 12, 14).

Meditation/Journal: What does the sign of water into wine mean to you? Where do you find the water of people's lives becoming wine?

Prayer: LORD God, when you brought your people out of Egypt, you worked mighty signs that they might believe in you. When Jesus, your Son, appeared on the earth, his sign of changing water into wine made him the groom for all bride-believers. Grant me the gift of faith that I may one day enjoy the eternal wedding with Jesus Christ, my Lord, who lives and reigns with you and the Holy Spirit, one God, forever and ever. Amen.

Conclusion

The most prominent image in the Bible is the vine or vineyard metaphor. It signifies Jerusalem, Judah, and Israel. When it refers to the whole nation of Israel, it gives the Israelites a sense of place. The song of the vineyard illustrates the elements of a vineyard. Usually planted on a hill, it had to be dug and the stones cleared and used to build a wall to protect it from wild animals. Then a watchtower was built from which a guard protected the vineyard from thieves. After the vines were planted a wine press was carved out of the stone, and a vat created to catch the pressed grapes at harvest time. Vinedressers cared for the vines and pruned them yearly. Once the vineyard metaphor is associated with Israel, God is understood to be the owner of the vineyard. The metaphor is further expanded into a love song, a place of rest, food for the poor, prosperity, and pleasure. After it becomes a sign of destruction, it emerges as a sign of restoration. Isaiah's song of the vineyard is the basis for the vineyard allegory (parable) of the tenants which shifts the identification from the land of Israel to God's kingdom as preached by Jesus of Nazareth. Underlying the allegory (parable) is the reason each evangelist thinks Jerusalem was destroyed by the Romans. By the end of the Bible, the vine and vineyard metaphor refers to the world; all people are invited to the messianic vineyard. Jesus himself becomes the new vine to which all the branches are connected. He also becomes the groom married to believers at the wedding, which signifies the union of all God's people.

Meditation/Journal: Which is your favorite vineyard story? Why? Does the vine and vineyard metaphor communicate to modern people the same way it did to ancient Jews and Christians? If so, how? If not, why not? When you see or buy grapes in the supermarket, what do you associate with them? When you drink wine, what do you associate with it?

Prayer: God of the vineyard, once you planted your people as choice vines on a fertile hill, building a watchtower, a wine press, and a vat. In later times, you revealed your Son, Jesus Christ, to be the true vine, from whom the branches get their life. Fill me with the life-giving energy of the Holy Spirit that I may safely arrive in the kingdom, where you live and reign as one God—Father, Son, and Holy Spirit—forever and ever. Amen.

2

Picking Grapes

Eating from One's Own Vine

Scripture: "During Solomon's lifetime Judah and Israel lived in safety ... under their vines." (1 Kgs 4:25)

Reflection: Before a person can pick grapes from the vines in his vineyard, he must have time to clear the land and plant the vines. This requires peace. The narrator of the First Book of Kings idealizes David's son, Solomon, as providing a time of tranquility so that the people of Judah and Israel were able to live in safety under their vines. The prophet Micah uses the same image after the destruction of Jerusalem and the Temple to offer hope for future restoration. Many people will "sit under their own vines" writes Micah (4:4), and they will "invite each other to come under [their] vine[s]" writes Zechariah (3:10). During the short period of independence enjoyed by the Jews in between Greek and Roman rulers, the author of the Second Book of Maccabees writes: "All the people sat under their own vines . . . , and there was none to make them afraid" (2 Macc 14:12). Thus, drinking a glass of wine offers one the opportunity to reflect upon the peace he or she enjoys whether one sits directly under the vines or not. With a glass of wine in hand, one can find a chair on a deck or in a sunroom, sitting in silence and being thankful for the tranquility in which one lives.

Meditation/Journal: Specifically, for what are you thankful?

Prayer: LORD God, grant peace to all peoples. Thank you for the tranquility that you have bestowed upon me. Make me evermore grateful for all your gifts, especially a glass of wine. Amen.

Dressing Vines

Scripture: "You shall plant vineyards and dress them, but you shall neither drink the wine nor gather the grapes, for the worm shall eat them." (Deut 28:39)

Reflection: A person who dresses vines or a vinedresser is one who cultivates, dresses, and prunes grape vines. Moses' words from the Book of Deuteronomy illustrate what will happen to the Israelites if they are disobedient to the Torah. In this specific case, Moses tells the people that the worm will eat the grapes on their planted, dressed, and pruned vines. The prophet Isaiah echoes this curse, stating that foreigners will dress Israel's vines (Isa 61:5). Technically, dressing vines refers to the summer process of trimming leaves away from grape clusters in order to expose them to the light. Pruning refers to the winter process of cutting away some of the branches to encourage fuller growth in the spring. A glass of wine can remind one of how this two-fold process is necessary for all of life. If some leaves—distractions, things, people—are not removed from life, full growth cannot occur. If some pruning—giving away, downsizing, dieting—is not done, new growth cannot take place.

Meditation/Journal: What dressing do you need to do in your life? What pruning do you need to do in your life?

Prayer: Heavenly Father, help me to know what needs to be dressed and what needs to be pruned in my life. Keep me safe from all harm. Amen.

Ripe Grapes

Scripture: " . . . [B]efore the harvest, when the blossom is over and the flower becomes a ripening grape, [the LORD] will cut off the shoots with pruning hooks, and the spreading branches he will hew away." (Isa 18:5)

Reflection: The prophet Isaiah compares the LORD to a wise farmer who patiently watches his vines bud and become ripe grapes before he prunes them. The ripe grapes are the people of Judah, whom God will gather, while the pruned shoots and branches are his people's enemies. Like a vinedresser snips the leaves on the vine after they have budded and produced grapes, God removes the enemies who threaten his chosen people. Later, the prophet describes the reduction of population by comparing it to "the gleaning when the grape harvest is ended" (Isa 24:13). Just as after the main grape harvest is complete and the last few grapes are gathered, so will these last few people, whom the LORD has rescued, praise him for saving them. The author of the OT (A) Book of Sirach employs Isaiah's words and applies them to wisdom: "From the first blossom to the ripening grape my heart delighted in [wisdom]" (Sir 51:15a). When the season of first ripe grapes (Num 13:20) arrives, the fruit is ready to be harvested. A glass of wine reminds a person of the budding and fruiting that had to precede the harvest. It also reminds a person of the patience required of the farmer before he harvests the crop.

Meditation/Journal: In your life, where is the budding and fruiting taking place that needs patience before the harvest?

Prayer: Almighty God, you patiently await the budding, growth, and ripe fruit of holiness in your people. Grant that I may be among those you harvest for eternity. Amen.

Clusters of Grapes

Scripture: The spies "cut down . . . a branch with a single cluster of grapes, and they carried it on a pole between two of them." (Num 13:23a)

Reflection: According to the HB (OT) Book of Numbers, the spies sent to see what was in the land of Canaan found a cluster of grapes so large that they had to hang it on a pole that rested on the shoulders of the two men bringing it back to the Israelite camp. Grapes also grew in Egypt as demonstrated by the Pharaoh's cupbearer's dream about a vine with three branches, each of which budded, blossomed, and developed into clusters of ripened grapes which the cupbearer squeezed into a cup of wine (Gen 40:9–11). And the author of the CB (NT) Book of Revelation narrates how the Son of Man is told by an angel to use his sharp sickle "and gather the clusters of the vine of the earth, for its grapes are ripe" (Rev 14:18). While it is not impossible for a single grape to grow on a vine, grapes usually grow in clusters. Each grape on the harvested cluster is squeezed of its juice so that no individual traits remain. Together the cluster of grapes form a glass of wine, something one grape cannot do. Thus, not only do the grapes grow in a unified cluster on a vine, but they enter into a greater unity when they have been squeezed together and fermented into wine.

Meditation/Journal: In what specific ways have you experienced yourself being like a grape in a cluster? What wine did you and others produce?

Prayer: Even though you create people as individuals, O LORD, you call them to work together for the growth of your kingdom. Grant me the strength to become the cup of wine that represents your work in the world now and forever. Amen.

Grape-Gatherer

Scripture: "Thus says the LORD of hosts: Glean thoroughly as a vine the remnant of Israel; like a grape-gatherer, pass your hand again over its branches." (Jer 6:9)

Reflection: When a person gleans, he or she goes over a vineyard that has just been harvested and gathers by hand any usable grapes that remain. The prophet Jeremiah records the LORD giving him such directions. He is to glean the remnant of Israel, that is, he is to gather those few people who have remained faithful to their God. Thus, there is the harvest, the first gleaning, and Jeremiah is to glean what God has already gleaned. Later in his book, Jeremiah uses the same analogy about a remnant, asking, "If grape-gatherers came . . . , would they not leave gleanings?" (Jer 49:9; Obad 1:5) The LORD's words to Jeremiah contradict his words to Moses: "When you gather the grapes of your vineyard, do not glean what is left; it shall be for the alien, the orphan, and the widow" (Deut 24:21). Ben Sira states that when it came to acquiring wisdom, he "was like a gleaner following the grape-pickers; by the blessing of the Lord [he] arrived first, and like a grape-picker [he] filled [his] wine press" (Sir 33:16–17); in other words, Ben Sira became one of the best and wisest teachers. Jesus exercises his role as a teacher, asking a crowd, "Are grapes gathered from thorns . . . ? (Matt 7:16) While Matthew records no answer to Jesus' question, the Lukan Jesus makes it clear that grapes are not picked from a bramble bush (Luke 6:44). A glass of wine represents the several gleanings of the grapes on the vines in the vineyard. The wise harvester lets nothing go to waste.

Meditation/Journal: Like a grape-gatherer, who has requested more from you that you didn't think you had at first? How were you stretched (squeezed)?

Prayer: LORD, you never cease to glean the remnant of those who place their trust in you. Pass your hand over me and call forth gifts that I didn't even know I had. Grant me the wisdom of Ben Sira and Jesus. Amen.

3

Processing Grapes

Treading Grapes

Scripture: "They went out into the field and gathered the grapes from their vineyards, trod them, and celebrated." (Judg 9:27)

Reflection: In the ancient world there were two stages to the processing of grapes. The first consisted of placing the grapes in a trough cut into rock; then, they were treaded with the feet. Nehemiah notes that he "saw in Judah people treading wine presses on the sabbath" (Neh 13:15). The juice that resulted from the treading of grapes (Mic 6:15) flowed from a drain to another trough cut into rock at a level lower than the first. The treading of grapes was a festive celebration. Isaiah notes that songs were sung and a "vintage-shout" was heard (Isa 16:10). Jeremiah notes that the treading was accompanied "with shouts of joy" (Jer 48:33). The prophet Amos envisions a time of restoration when the "the treader of grapes [will overtake] the one who sows the seed" (Amos 9:13a). The treading of grapes with feet, while it may not appeal to modern people, brings the person and the grapes into close contact with each other. Furthermore, the treading takes place in a rock trough, which places people, grapes, and earth in conjunction with each other. This helps to explain the earthy aroma of a good wine.

Meditation/Journal: What celebration accompanies your drinking of a glass of wine? How does the drinking of a glass of wine connect you to the earth?

Prayer: While they tread the grapes, your people rejoice in your blessings, O LORD. Grant that I might celebrate your blessings when I drink wine and renew my connection to the earth and everything you have made. Amen.

Wine Press

Scripture: "Gladness and joy have been taken away from the fruitful land . . . ; I have stopped the wine from the wine presses; no one treads them with shouts of joy. . . . " (Jer 48:33)

Reflection: As noted above, the first stage of processing grapes is treading them with feet. The second stage occurs in the second cut rock trough into which has flowed the grape juice. Now, the grapes are pressed by means of a beam weighted with a stone or some other heavy object. As punishment, God declares through the prophet Jeremiah that he has stopped the wine from flowing from the wine presses. The Book of Deuteronomy mentions wine presses (Deut 16:13) as do the HB (OT) books of Judges (6:11; 7:25), the Second Book of Kings (6:27), and Job (24:11). The prophet Zechariah mentions "the king's wine presses," which served as a boundary marker (Zech 14:10). After the grapes are trod, they need further pressing in order to get out of them all their juice. Most of the tasks of life require a further pressing, that is, more attention to detail, going over the project a second time, reiterating the directions, etc. In order to get most out of one's self, more pressing may be required.

Meditation/Journal: What experience in your life needed further pressing to become a success? How does a glass of wine remind you of this need for a second pressing?

Prayer: The gladness and joy that accompany the pressing of grapes remind me of your goodness, LORD God. When I am not giving one hundred percent of my life to you, stop the wine press and remind me of the joy that comes with total commitment. Amen.

4

Types of Wine

Sweet Wine

Scripture: [Nehemiah said to the people,] "Go your way, eat the fat and drink sweet wine and send portions of them to those for whom nothing is prepared, for this day is holy to our LORD; and do not be grieved, for the joy of the LORD is your strength." (Neh 8:10)

Reflection: Sweet, when it comes to wine, means tasting or smelling sugary. Such a designation is the opposite of dry, lacking the sugary taste or smell. According to the prophets Joel and Amos, on the day the LORD restores Jerusalem "the mountains shall drip sweet wine" (Joel 3:18b; Amos 9:13b). The OT (HB) Book of Esther refers to "the royal wine" in the court of King Ahasuerus of Susa (Esth 1:7). Nehemiah's exhortation to the people—after they heard the reading of the Book of Law—to celebrate the holy day with sweet wine associates the drink with the joy of the LORD, who is his people's strength. Thus, there is a specialness attached to sweet wine. Drinking of glass of either red or white sweet wine can remind one that his or her strength comes from God. Just as one drinks sweet wine, one also drinks of God's sweet promises.

Meditation/Journal: Do you prefer sweet or dry wines? If you prefer sweet, with what do you associate the sweetness? If dry, with what do you associate the dryness?

Prayer: At your coming, LORD God, the mountains drip sweet wine. Grant me the strength to one day share in the joy of your kingdom. Amen.

Sour Wine

Scripture: "A jar full of sour wine was standing [near Jesus' cross]. So [the soldiers] put a sponge full of the wine on a branch of hyssop and held it to his mouth. When Jesus had received the wine, he said, 'It is finished.' Then he bowed his head and gave up his spirit." (John 19:29–30)

Reflection: Only the author of John's Gospel mentions the detail of the soldiers giving Jesus a sponge soaked in sour wine at the end of a branch of hyssop. The detail is meant to tie Jesus' death into that of the passover lamb, whose blood was smeared on the doorposts and lintel of the Hebrews' homes in Egypt with hyssop (Exod 12:22). Sour wine possesses a sharp or tart acidic taste; it provokes Jesus to declare that the marriage of God and people is finished and then bow his head and die. The author of Mark's Gospel notes an unidentified person who "filled a sponge with sour wine, put it on a stick, and gave it to [Jesus] to drink" (Mark 15:36). Matthew and Luke, both of whom used Mark as a source for their gospels, write the same, although only Luke mentions that the soldiers offered Jesus sour wine (Matt 27:48; Luke 23:36). Sour wine is associated with the tartness of death in the CB's (NT's) narratives about Jesus' dying on the cross. And sour wine is associated with the sharp events that occur in lives today.

Meditation/Journal: With what event in your life do you associate sour wine? Explain.

Prayer: The death of your Son on the cross, Father, was like sour wine. Give me the strength to persevere through the acidic events of my life. I ask this through Jesus Christ, my Lord. Amen.

Common Wine

Scripture: Holofernes commanded his servants "to bring [Judith] in where his silver dinnerware was kept, and ordered them to set a table for her with some of his own delicacies, and with some of his own wine to drink." (Jdt 12:1)

Reflection: Common drinking wine, like that prepared for Judith by Holofernes's servants, is what today is called table wine, box wine, or house wine. Instead of being served out of a bottle, table wine and house wine are drained from a large container—such as a cask—into a carafe from which the wine is poured into a glass. While common wine is usually cheaper, it does not mean that it is inferior to wine poured from a bottle. In the OT (A) Book of Judith, Holofernes—King Nebuchadnezzar's army general—attempts to seduce Judith, a young, widowed, Jewish woman, with common wine. However, he ends up drinking "a great quantity of wine, much more than he had ever drunk in any one day since he was born" (Jdt 12:20), and while he is sleeping it off, she draws his sword and assassinates him by cutting off his head (Jdt 13:13:6-10). Thus, she saves her people from their enemy. Like Judith, there is Esther, who also saves her people after drinking common wine (Add Esth 5:6; 7:2). Thus, common wine can enable ordinary women to become heroines.

Meditation/Journal: What does drinking common wine empower you to do?

Prayer: Father in heaven, with common wine you strengthen your servants to become heroines of your people and save them from death. Set a table for me with some delicacies and wine to drink in your kingdom. Amen.

New Wine

Scripture: "[W]hat goodness and beauty are [the LORD's]! Grain shall make the young men flourish, and new wine the young women." (Zech 9:17)

Reflection: After the grape harvest in the Beaujolais region of France in the fall of every year, signs begin to appear announcing that the new Beaujolais wine, made from Gamay grapes, is ready. The wine is fermented for just a few weeks before it is bottled and goes on sale, usually on the third Thursday of November. What the French call *Beaujolais nouveau* the Bible names *new* in Zechariah's bucolic, pastoral imagery concerning young men and women. The prophet Hosea thinks that new wine takes away understanding (Hos 4:11), but he also compares the restoration of his people to the blossoming of the vine and the fragrance of the wine of Lebanon (Hos 14:7). Ben Sira thinks that the drinking of such new wine should be accompanied with the melody of music (Sir 32:6), while the prophet Haggai records the LORD declaring a drought on the new wine until his house in Jerusalem is rebuilt (Hag 1:11). In Luke's Gospel, Jesus states that "no one after drinking old wine desires new wine" (Luke 5:39), and in the Acts of the Apostles, the apostles are accused of being "filled with new wine" on Pentecost (Acts 2:13b). While a glass of new wine may not contain the refined taste of an aged one, it can remind the drinker that some things need to be done quickly. Paraphrasing the old Ernest and Julio Gallo commercials, some wine needs to be sold before its time!

Meditation/Journal: Recently, what have you had to do without a lot of planning? How is that like drinking new wine?

Prayer: What goodness and beauty are yours, O LORD! You provide food and new wine so your people flourish in your sight. Make me grateful for all your gifts now and forever. Amen.

Wine Mixed with Water

Scripture: " ... [J]ust as it is harmful to drink wine alone, or, again, to drink water alone, while wine mixed with water is sweet and delicious and enhances one's enjoyment, so also the style of the story delights the ears of those who read the work." (2 Macc 15:39a)

Reflection: The OT (A) Second Book of Maccabees notes the harm of drinking wine without cutting it with water for the taste in the mouth as a metaphor for hearing (or reading) a good story in one's ears. Because of the consistency of the grape juice that was fermented into wine in the ancient world, it was necessary to dilute the thick wine with some water both to drink it and to enjoy it. It may also have been flavored with spices. The HB (OT) Book of Proverbs portrays personified wisdom as mixing wine (Prov 9:2, 5) as does the prophet Isaiah (1:22; 65:11). In its wise words section, Proverbs explains that "[t]hose who linger late over wine, those who keep trying mixed wines," have red eyes (Prov 23:30). While most wine connoisseurs would never think of opening an aged bottle of Malbec and cutting it with water today, there are a few people who might add an ice cube to it to cool it! That action alone is enough to make cringe one who appreciates the aromas of fine wine.

Meditation/Journal: How is your life like wine mixed with water? Explain. How is your life like wine mixed with spices? Explain.

Prayer: Your words, eternal God, delight the ears of those who hear and read them. Give me the insight to understand how they articulate the experiences of my life that are like wine mixed with water. All praise be yours now and forever. Amen.

Types of Wine

Wine Mixed with Myrrh

Scripture: "[The soldiers] offered [Jesus] wine mixed with myrrh; but he did not take it." (Mark 15:23)

Reflection: In the account of Jesus' crucifixion in Mark's Gospel, the soldiers offer Jesus wine mixed with myrrh before they crucify him. Wine mixed with myrrh, a spice produced from the gum resin of a large bush or small tree, creates a sedative which brings the person who takes it to a state of calm, much like an anesthetic works today. According to Mark, who focuses on Jesus' suffering, he refuses the drink. However, in Matthew's Gospel the soldiers offer Jesus "wine to drink, mixed with gall; but when he tasted it, he would not drink it" (Matt 27:34). In Matthew's Gospel, Jesus tastes the mixture before he refuses to drink it. What is Mark's narcotic becomes a cruel, bitter drink in Matthew. According to Luke's unique parable, the good Samaritan poured wine on the wounds of the man beaten by robbers (Luke 10:24), identifying another use for wine as a soothing external medication. While today most people would take a prescribed sedative or an over-the-counter pain-pill killer without ever thinking of pouring wine over any kind of flesh wound, in the biblical world mixed wine was all people had to dull pain.

Meditation/Journal: How can wine be used as a narcotic? Should wine-drinkers be cognizant of the addictive quality of alcohol to dull pain? Where do you draw the line between wine-enjoyment and wine-addiction?

Prayer: In your great mercy, O LORD, you gave wine mixed with myrrh to your people to dull the pain of their suffering. Grant that I may never abuse your gift of wine, but, rather, praise your compassion now and forever. Amen.

5

Storage of Wine

Vat

Scripture: "Honor the LORD with your substance and with the first fruits of all your produce; then . . . your vats will be bursting with wine." (Prov 3:9–10)

Reflection: After the grapes were tread and pressed, the juice was placed into a vat, which Isaiah indicates was hewed out of rock (Isa 5:2). If the rock were solid, the grape juice could be placed in it like one puts liquid in a bowl. If the rock were porous, the vat may be plastered to seal it and keep the grape juice from seeping into the ground. The prophet Hosea mentions a wine vat (Hos 9:2), while the prophet Joel describes vats overflowing with wine (Joel 2:24; 3:13). The grape juice fermented in the vat for at least six weeks. The HB (OT) Book of Proverbs stipulates that honoring the LORD with one's wealth and fulfilling the law of offering first fruits as thanksgiving to God will result in vats full of wine. Thus, the vat—today the tank or barrel—represents abundance that must be divided and shared. One never drinks a glass of wine alone; the wine is part of a greater amount of which many people share.

Meditation/Journal: When drinking a glass of wine, with whom are you sharing? To whom are you connected?

Prayer: You make the vine produce abundant grapes, O LORD, which, when trod, pressed, and fermented become wine. Accept my thanksgiving for this great gift, and through the wine I drink, keep me connected to you both now and forever. Amen.

Skins

Scripture: Jesus said: "[N]o one puts new wine into old wineskins; otherwise, the wine will burst the skins, and the wine is lost, and so are the skins; but one puts new wine into fresh wineskins." (Mark 2:22)

Reflection: After wine ferments in a vat, it is often stored and transported in a skin. The skin is the hide of a goat that has been sewed in such a way as to form a container with a stopper at its narrowest point. However, wine continues to ferment, and it releases gases that expand in the closed space of a wineskin. Thus, Jesus' words about new wine bursting brittle, old, goat skins are true. Then, both wine and skins are lost. The proper procedure for storing new wine is to put it into new wineskins that are flexible enough to expand. Both the author of Matthew's Gospel and the author of Luke's Gospel preserve Jesus' words found in Mark (Matt 9:17; Luke 5:37-38). In the HB (OT) Book of Job, Elihu captures the idea when he states that his heart is "like wine that has no vent; like new wineskins, it is ready to burst" (Job 32:19). The HB (OT) First Book of Samuel mentions skins of wine (1 Sam 1:24; 10:3; 16:20; 25:18) as do the Second Book of Samuel (16:1-2), the Book of Nehemiah (5:18), and the OT (A) Book of Judith (10:5). Today, the wine bottle with its cork serves the same purpose as the wineskin once did; the cork permits the gasses to escape so the bottle does not explode, and it permits easy transport of the precious liquid.

Meditation/Journal: How are you like a wineskin—either old or new?

Prayer: Almighty God, you do not pour your Spirit into old wineskins, but are forever at work recreating your people anew so that the Spirit may expand them with your grace. Grant me the gift of flexibility that I might be a worthy container for renewed life now and forever. Amen.

Wine Jar

Scripture: "You shall speak to [the people of Judah] this word: Thus says the LORD, the God of Israel: Every wine-jar should be filled with wine. And they will say to you, 'Do you think we do not know that every wine-jar should be filled with wine?'" (Jer 13:12)

Reflection: A vessel larger than a skin for storing wine is called a wine-jar or an amphora. Such jars were made of fired clay and featured two handles for carrying and pointed ends which enabled the jar to be stuck into the earth to keep the wine cool. After the wine was drained from the vat into the jar, the jar was sealed with clay and the owner's name or seal was stamped into it. A small hole near one of the handles permitted gasses to escape without destroying the jar. Any sediment would settle to the bottom of the jar, which was tipped to the side to pour the wine into serving pitchers, decanters, or wineskins. The prophet Jeremiah writes about filling wine-jars (Jer 13:12), about dregs that settle from the wine, about emptying wine from one vessel to another (Jer 48:11), about decanters into which the wine in the jars is poured, and about breaking wine-jars (Jer 48:12). Today, wine-jars or amphora are no longer used; however, along side of the standard .20 gallon bottle are the Rehoboam (1.1 gallons), the Methuselah (1.5 gallons), the Salamanazar (2.38 gallons), the Balthazar (3.17 gallons), and the Nebuchadnezzar (3.9 gallons), to name but a few of the larger bottles.

Meditation/Journal: How are you like a wine-jar? How large are you? Why kind of wine do you contain?

Prayer: Heavenly Father, you fill your people with the breath of life, like one fills a jar with wine. Grant that the spiritual fermentation that occurs in me will result in eternal life. Amen.

Vessel

Scripture: "Under the influence of . . . wine, [King] Belshazzar commanded that [his lords] bring in the vessels of gold and silver that his father Nebuchadnezzar had taken out of the temple in Jerusalem, so that the king and his lords, his wives, and his concubines might drink from them. So they brought in the vessels of gold and silver that had been taken out of the temple, the house of God in Jerusalem, and the king and his lords, his wives, and his concubines drank from them." (Dan 5:2-3)

Reflection: While the writer of the story above did not know that Belshazzar was the son of Nabonidus and that he was never a king, the purpose of the story remains: the sacrilegious act of drinking wine from the holy vessels pillaged from the Jerusalem temple by Nebuchadnezzar, king of Babylon (Dan 1:2; 2 Kgs 24:13; 25:14-15; Ezra 1:7-11). Vessel refers to a container made of wood, stone, bronze, iron, gold, silver, and usually clay holding various amounts. Earthen vessels could be fired with or without a glaze. The vessels commissioned by King Solomon and used in the Jerusalem temple were made of hammered gold and silver. Belshazzar's sacrilege, according to Daniel, is the drinking of wine from them by Belshazzar, his lords, his wives, and his concubines and not honoring the "the God in whose power is [his] very breath" (Dan 5:23). Some churches maintain sacred vessels made of a variety of substances, but often gold and silver. Some homes contain vessels for drinking wine that are used only on special occasions. Thus, there is something within humankind that preserves some vessels for celebrations that are deemed extraordinary.

Meditation/Journal: What common vessels for drinking wine do you own? What special vessels for drinking wine do you own? When are the special vessels used?

Prayer: O LORD, you directed that special vessels of gold and silver be made to serve you in your house in Jerusalem. Grant that I may be one of your worthy servants, serving you now on earth and one day in heaven. Amen.

Storehouses for Wine

Scripture: "[King] Hezekiah had very great riches and honor; and he made for himself . . . storehouses . . . for the yield of . . . wine. . . . " (2 Chr 32:27–28)

Reflection: Jars or amphorae of wine need to be stored. King Hezekiah of Jerusalem built storehouses, buildings into which he placed his wine. Before Hezekiah, Solomon sent large amounts of wine from his storehouses to King Huram of Tyre as payment to lumberjacks for timber to build the temple (2 Chr 2:10, 15), and Solomon's son, Rehoboam, supplied his fortresses with stores of wine (2 Chr 11:11). Also, storehouses were built to hold tithes of wine from the Israelites and Jews (2 Chr 31:5; Neh 13:5, 12). The modern equivalent to a storehouse is a wine cellar or a wine cave. Vineyards that process grapes have underground or partially underground storage facilities where tanks, casks, and bottles of wine are kept cool. Any dark, cool room can be used to store bottles of wine. While these may be located in a basement, modern wine cellars with climate control often resembling refrigerators come in a variety of shapes and sizes and can be placed anywhere in one's home.

Storage of Wine

Meditation/Journal: Where do you store wine to keep it out of the light and cool? How are you and that dark, cool place alike and united when you open a bottle of wine and drink a glass of it?

Prayer: Out of your abundance, O LORD, you enable your people to fill storehouses with wine. Grant that the wine I drink may make me aware of your blessings and lead me to praise you now and forever. Amen.

6

Measuring and Tasting Wine

A Bath

Scripture: "Solomon sent word to King Huram of Tyre: 'I will provide for your servants, those who cut the timber, . . . twenty thousand baths of wine. . . .'" (2 Chr 2:3, 10)

Reflection: When it comes to measuring wine, most people know that a standard wine bottle holds seven hundred fifty milliliters or .20 gallons. About five glasses of wine can be poured from a standard bottle of wine. Furthermore, when reading the phrase *bath of wine*, most people would think of soaking in a tub filled with wine. However, a biblical bath of wine consisted of a little over six gallons. Solomon pays the lumberjacks with twenty thousand baths of wine; that equals more than one hundred twenty thousand gallons of wine! Likewise, King Artaxerxes issues the priest-scribe Ezra up to "one hundred baths of wine" (Ezra 7:22), which is more than six hundred gallons of wine. A bath of wine was subdivided into six hins, each hin consisting of a just a little over a gallon. The universal standardization of measures remains a hope for the future, as most countries have a set of standard measures, but they differ from other countries around the world. So, when pouring a glass of wine, one might wish that it were a hin rather than one hundred fifty milliliters or .04 gallon.

Meditation/Journal: How do you measure spiritual growth in your life? How does that method compare or contrast to how you measure wine?

Prayer: Your mercy, O LORD, is beyond measure. As I experience your grace going before me and following after, help me to realize your generosity and to praise you forever. Amen.

A Measure

Scripture: "Now the Babylonians had an idol called Bel, and every day they provided for it . . . six measures of wine." (Dan 14:3 [Bel 1:3])

Reflection: The story of Bel in the OT (A) Book of Daniel mentions that the idol was provided six measures of wine every day which was consumed by the seventy priests of Bel, their wives, and children when they entered the temple through a secret passage. A liquid measure consisted of ten baths or about sixty and a half gallons. In other words, three hundred sixty-three gallons of wine were offered to Bel every day! The prophet Hosea writes about bringing one measure of wine to an adulteress the LORD instructs him to marry (Hos 3:2); that one measure is over sixty and half gallons of wine! Modern people, who are used to measuring wine by the seven-hundred-fifty-milliliter bottle, may have some difficulty conceptualizing these huge amounts of wine which, today, are found only in wineries. In wine cellars, large amounts of wine are kept in fermenting and storage tanks and in casks and barrels. Even after visiting a winery and seeing the size of the tanks

51

and barrels, modern people tend to think in more manageable amounts.

Meditation/Journal: What is your paradigm for measuring—teaspoon, tablespoon, cup, pint, quart, gallon? Can how your paradigm for measuring be applied to your spiritual life?

Prayer: Ever-living God, who gives me gifts beyond measure, grant that I may be as generous with others as you have been with the gifts you have given to me. May a good measure, pressed down, shaken together, running over, be placed in my hands now and forever. Amen.

Tasting Wine

Scripture: " . . . [I]n the twentieth year of King Artaxerxes, when wine was served him, I [, Nehemiah,] carried the wine and gave it to the king." (Neh 2:1a)

Reflection: The task Nehemiah mentions was often referred to as serving as the cupbearer. The patriarch Joseph accurately interprets Pharaoh's chief cupbearer's dream in the HB (OT) Book of Genesis (40:9–13). In royal households, like that in which Nehemiah and Pharaoh's chief cupbearer served, the cupbearer poured wine, and in some situations tasted it to be sure it was good or not poisoned. According to the Second Book of Chronicles, King David appointed "over the produce of the vineyards for the wine cellars . . . Zabdi the Shiphmite" (1 Chr 27:27b). Today such tasks are performed by a sommelier, a wine steward in a restaurant, hotel, or other establishment, who supervises the ordering, storing, and serving of wine. He or she may be recognized by the small mental cup dangling from a chain around his or her neck which is used to see the color of the wine and to taste it. The author of the HB (OT) Book of Proverbs ill advises: "Do not look at wine when it is red, when it sparkles in the cup and goes down smoothly" (Prov 23:31). Indeed, such a wine is ready to be served and consumed!

Measuring and Tasting Wine

Meditation/Journal: What does your role as a sommelier teach you about your spirituality, especially your responsibility to order, store, and serve wine?

Prayer: Heavenly Father, only you can make of me a worthy cupbearer in your service. Grant me the grace to know you and to serve you by knowing others who know and serve you now and forever. Amen.

7

Wine with Food

Bread and Wine

Scripture: " . . . King Melchizedek of Salem brought out bread and wine; he was priest of God Most High." (Gen 14:18)

Reflection: Contrary to many understandings, Melchizedek of Jerusalem is a Canaanite king and priest of a god named *God Most High*, who is not the same as the LORD, who is often referred to with the same title. Bread and wine serve as an offering of thanksgiving by Melchizedek to Abram, who helped defeat other kings who had attacked him. Bread and wine are food staples of most cultures (Judg 19:19; Lam 2:12). Bread is easy to make from wheat, barley, rice, etc; wine is a necessity where water is unsafe for drinking. Ancient people drank wine because it was safe, like modern people drink purified water because it is safe. Even when celebrating Passover, Hebrews, Israelites, and Jews made unleavened bread—as a reminder that there had been no time to leaven the dough in the haste of leaving Egypt and because leaven or yeast was considered corrupt—and made thanksgiving to God with four cups of red wine. Bread and wine may no longer be considered a modern staple for sustaining life, but bread and water still are.

Meditation/Journal: What do you consider the staples of life to be today? How do those connect to the staples of your spiritual life?

Prayer: LORD, God Most High, you feed your people with bread and wine. Fill me with gratitude for your gifts, and sustain my life with your grace now and forever. Amen.

Eating and Drinking

Scripture: "One day when [Job's] sons and daughter were eating and drinking wine in the eldest brother's house, a messenger came to Job. . . . While he was still speaking, another came and said, 'Your sons and daughters were eating and drinking wine in their eldest brother's house, and suddenly a great wind came across the desert, struck the four corners of the house, and it fell on the young people. . . . " (Job 1:13-14, 18-19)

Reflection: As people are portrayed in the HB (OT) Book of Job, eating and drinking wine is a common occurrence. Such eating and drinking was done while sitting on the floor around a common pot or tray of food or while reclining on couches arranged around short tables. When Jacob is tricking his father Isaac out of his brother Esau's birthright, Jacob brings his father game and wine to drink (Gen 27:25). The prophet Isaiah, too, mentions "eating meat and drinking wine" (Isa 22:13); he promises destruction to those "who are heroes in drinking wine and valiant at mixing drink" (Isa 5:22). But it is the prophet Amos, who vehemently pronounces judgment on those who "drink wine bought with fines they imposed" (Amos 2:8) and "who drink wine from bowls" (Amos 6:6). He does offer a little hope that one day the Jews "shall plant vineyards and drink their wine" (Amos 9:14b). Today, drinking wine may take place before a meal while people engage in conversation, during the meal, or after the meal. Sometimes just sitting and sipping a glass of wine while reading a good book is enough.

Meditation/Journal: How often do you enjoy a glass of wine? Do you drink it without a meal, before a meal, during a meal, or after a meal? In what specific ways does the drinking of wine reflect your spiritual life?

Prayer: Ever-living God, you grace me with the gift of wine and the family bonds and friendships that result from sharing it. Grant that it may also bring me closer to you now and forever. Amen.

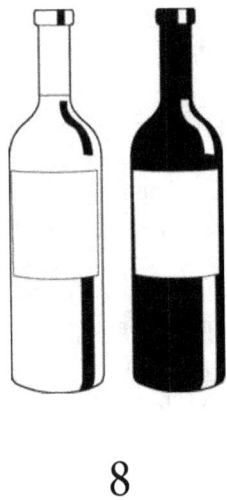

8

Effects of Wine

Gladness

Scripture: "O LORD my God, you are very great. You cause . . . wine to gladden the human heart. . . . " (Ps 104:1a, 14a, 15a)

Reflection: God provides. That is the message of Psalm 104, which offers a poetic list of all that God provides, including wine that gladdens the human heart (Zech 10:7). In Jotham's fable, the vine, which is asked to rule over the trees, asks in turn, "Shall I stop producing my wine that cheers gods and mortals . . . ?" (Judg 9:13) In Psalm 4, the singer tells the LORD, "You have put gladness in my heart more than when . . . wine abound[s]" (Ps 4:7). Likewise, Bagoas, Holofernes's eunuch in charge of his personal affairs, invites Judith "to enjoy drinking wine" (Jdt 12:13). Ben Sira gets right to the point, writing that "wine and music gladden the heart" (Sir 40:20). Gladness, joy, or cheer is a state of being delighted, happy, and pleased; gladness is an effect of drinking wine. The best gladness overflows into gratefulness to God for providing all that is needed and causing delight, happiness, and pleasure in all his creatures. The wine that gladdens the human heart is a feeling of cheerfulness and hopefulness in God's presence.

Meditation/Journal: In what specific ways does wine gladden your heart so that it results in gratefulness?

Prayer: O LORD my God, you demonstrate your greatness in providing for all your creatures. Thank you for the gift of wine which gladdens my heart, and grant that I may never cease to praise you in gratitude now and forever. Amen.

Cheer

Scripture: "I searched with my mind how to cheer my body with wine—my mind still guiding me with wisdom—and how to lay hold on folly, until I might see what was good for mortals to do under heaven during the few days of their life." (Eccl 2:3)

Reflection: The author of the HB (OT) Book of Ecclesiastes offers observations based on human experience and interprets these wisely knowing that death is inevitable. In between birth and death is life, but a person can never know exactly the meaning of life. Since this limited understanding affects everyone, all a person can do is enjoy life and the experiences that form it, especially the experience of drinking wine. One of the writer's observations consists of the cheer wine brings to his body. He tells the reader: "Go, eat your bread with enjoyment, and drink your wine with a merry heart, for God has long ago approved what you do" (Eccl 9:7), and he adds "wine gladdens life" (Eccl 10:19). Cheer, a state of well-being and optimism, is the most for which one can hope during life, according to Ecclesiastes. The author of the OT (A) Book of Sirach puts the same idea this way: "Wine drunk at the proper time and in moderation is rejoicing of heart and gladness of soul" (Sir 31:28). In the words of the prophet Jeremiah, people can "be radiant over the goodness of the LORD, over the ... wine, ... and they shall never languish again" (Jer 31:12).

Meditation/Journal: In what specific ways does drinking wine result in a state of well-being and optimism for you?

Prayer: You have made wine to cheer my heart, LORD God, and to instill in me a state of well-being and optimism. Guide me with your wisdom and reveal to me what is good to do under heaven during the few days of my life. Make me radiant over your goodness now and forever. Amen.

Bitterness

Scripture: "Wine is a mocker, strong drink a brawler, and whoever is led astray by it is not wise." (Prov 20:1)

Reflection: Wine can treat a person with scorn or contempt. Other strong drink can cause rough and noisy fights. Both can lead to bitterness. The OT (A) Book of Sirach echoes these sentiments: "Wine drunk to excess leads to bitterness of spirit, to quarrels and stumbling" (Sir 31:29). Thus, one should "not try to prove ... strength by wine-drinking, for wine has destroyed many" (Sir 31:25). The prophet Isaiah, too, addresses the mocking bitterness in the community caused by wine when he records people saying: "Come, let us get wine; let us fill ourselves with strong drink" (Isa 56:12a). Bitterness, the state in which one expresses intense hostility, can be the result of being "overcome with wine" (Isa 28:1). Likewise, the psalmist compares God's awakening to defend his people in Judah to that of "a warrior shouting because of wine" (Ps 78:65). In other words, too much wine leads to bitterness, a hostile state that can destroy a person.

Meditation/Journal: Have you ever experienced bitterness as a result of drinking too much wine? In what types of hostile behavior was it manifest? What do you learn from reflecting on these experiences?

Prayer: Do not let me be led astray by wine-drinking, almighty God. Rather, remove the bitterness from my life and help me to beg forgiveness from those I may have wronged when influenced by strong drink. Hear this petition. Amen.

Drunkenness

Scripture: "My heart is crushed within me, all my bones shake; I have become like a drunkard, like one overcome by wine, because of the LORD and because of his holy words." (Jer 23:9)

Reflection: Another effect of wine is drunkenness. The prophet Jeremiah compares the state of the prophet in receiving God's words to that of a drunkard. Just like the drunkard experiences a disordered state of mind which leaves him shaken and befuddled, so does the prophet's experience of ecstatic intuition (parapsychological experience) makes him look like he is drunk! Drunkenness results in loss of control over behavior, movement—reeling and staggering (Ps 60:3; Isa 28:7)—and speech. Isaiah uses the same image to describe people's inability to discern God's purpose: "Be drunk, but not from wine: stagger, but not from strong drink!" (Isa 29:9) In describing the effect that the nation of Babylon had on the world, Jeremiah employs the image of drunkenness again: "Babylon was a golden cup in the LORD's hand, making all the earth drunken; the nations drank of her wine, and so the nations went mad" (Jer 51:7). The first biblical person to become drunk is Noah (Gen 9:21). He is followed by Lot, whose daughters get him drunk on wine, sleep with him, and conceive children (Gen 19:30–38). Thus, drunkenness can result in the lack of self-control.

Meditation/Journal: Have you ever experienced a state of ecstatic intuition or divine revelation? To what would you compare it?

Prayer: Like wine can leave me without control of behavior, movement, or speech, your words, O God, can crush my heart within me and make my bones shake. Keep me ever attentive to your revelation now and forever. Amen.

EFFECTS OF WINE

Merriment

Scripture: "... Absalom commanded his servants, 'Watch when Amnon's heart is merry with wine, and when I say to you, "Strike Amnon," then kill him. Do not be afraid; have I not myself commanded you? Be courageous and valiant.'" (2 Sam 13:28)

Reflection: After preparing a feast, Absalom, one of King David's sons, watches his brother, Amnon, become merry with wine, and commands his servants to kill him in revenge for having raped his sister, Tamar. Likewise, Holofernes drinks a great quantity of wine, becoming merry, and Judith cuts off his head with his sword (Jdt 12:16—13:10). Esther's opportunity to become queen in Ahasuerus's court comes as a result of the king being merry with wine and summoning Queen Vashti, who refuses his command (Esth 1:10-12). The prophet Isaiah refers to the state of being merry with wine as being inflamed by wine (Isa 5:11), and the prophet Hosea calls it the heat of wine (Hos 7:5). The author of the CB (NT) Letter to the Ephesians calls it debauchery, unrestrained self-indulgence (Eph 5:18). Likewise, the author of the CB (NT) Book of Revelation refers to Rome's wine of fornication—sexual intercourse outside marriage—drunk by the inhabitants of the earth (Rev 17:2). Thus while drinking wine in moderation is good, becoming merry with wine results in rape, death, loss of position, and self-indulgence.

Meditation/Journal: Have you ever been merry with wine? What were the results?

Prayer: Loving Father, giver of the vineyard, the vine, and the wine, preserve me from all merriment and its results from drinking wine. Instill in me a great appreciation for this gift now and forever. Amen.

9

No Wine-Drinking

Nazirites

Scripture: "The LORD spoke to Moses, saying: Speak to the Israelites and say to them: When either men or women make a special vow, the vow of a nazirite, to separate themselves to the LORD, they shall separate themselves from wine and strong drink; ... and [they] shall not drink any grape juice or eat grapes, fresh or dried. All their days as nazirites they shall eat nothing that is produced by the grapevine, not even the seeds or the skins." (Num 6:1–4)

Reflection: A nazirite, either man or woman, was a person who made a special vow to offer himself or herself in service to the LORD for a specified, that is, a limited duration (Num 6:20). Manoah's unnamed wife is directed by the angel of the LORD to be a nazirite during her pregnancy (Judg 13:4, 7, 14), and her son, Samson, is to be a life-long nazirite (Judg 13:5, 7). Likewise, in her prayer to the LORD asking him for a son, Hannah, who has "drunk neither wine nor strong drink" (1 Sam 1:15), promises that if she conceives and gives birth to a son that she will dedicate him as a life-long nazirite (1 Sam 1:11). The prophet Amos reminds the Israelites that the LORD raised some of their youths to be nazirites (Amos 2:11a), but the people made them drink wine (Amos 2:12). In the CB (NT), the author of Luke's Gospel presents John the Baptist as a nazirite (Luke 1:15, 7:33); he drank no wine or strong drink. While no one refers to himself or herself today as being a nazirite, there are people who do not drink wine or strong drink for a variety of reasons; both they and their reasons should be respected.

Meditation/Journal: Have you ever stopped drinking wine or strong drink for a period of time, such as during Lent, as a devotional act? What were the results?

Prayer: You often call people to refrain from drinking wine or strong drink in order to be devoted only to you, O LORD. Grant that my abstinence may praise you as well as my imbibing and draw me closer to you now and forever. Amen.

Ministry

Scripture: " . . . [T]he LORD spoke to Aaron: Drink no wine or strong drink, neither you nor your sons, when you enter the tent of meeting, that you may not die; it is a statue forever throughout your generations." (Lev 10:8–9)

Reflection: So that they could exercise their priestly duties responsibly and instruct the people carefully, Aaron and his sons are forbidden wine and strong drink before exercising their ministry. Thus, in addition to the nazirites, the priests may not drink wine before fulfilling their duties. The prophet Ezekiel, when detailing the regulations concerning the new temple, states, "No priest shall drink wine when he enters the inner court" of the sanctuary (Ezek 44:21). These rules may be behind the statement about deacons "not indulging in much wine" in the First Letter to Timothy (3:8) in the CB (NT) and in the Letter to Titus about bishops not being addicted to wine (Titus 1:7). However, the author of First Timothy does tell him, "No longer drink only water, but take a little wine for the sake of your stomach and your frequent ailments" (1 Tim 5:23). This latter directive may be based on Tobit's words in the OT (A) book of the same name to his son Tobias: "Do not drink wine to excess or let drunkenness go with you on your way" (Tob 4:15b).

Meditation/Journal: Why is it important for you to approach responsibilities without drinking wine?

Prayer: LORD, you spoke to Aaron, telling him and his sons not to drink wine before entering the tent of meeting to worship you. Fill me with the wisdom not to share strong drink as I go about the responsibilities of my day that I may praise you with clear mind, heart, and soul. Amen.

Rechabites

Scripture: " . . . I [, Jeremiah,] set before the Rechabites pitchers full of wine, and cups; and I said to them, 'Have some wine.' But they answered, 'We will drink no wine, for our ancestor . . . Rechab commanded us, "You shall never drink wine, neither you nor your children."'" (Jer 35:5-6)

Reflection: While only the prophet Jeremiah mentions the Rechabites, their ancestor Rechab is mentioned eight times in the HB (OT) (2 Sam 4:2, 5, 6, 9; 2 Kgs 10:15, 23; 1 Chr 2:55; Neh 3:14). The Rechabites, a nomad clan, worshiped the LORD, but they did not drink wine probably because they moved from place to place and viticulture requires stability. "We have no vineyard," they tell Jeremiah (35:9) after he gathers a group of them and offers them wine, but they refuse to drink it. Their loyalty to the LORD is then contrasted by the prophet to Israel's disloyalty, and the LORD promises blessings to the house of the Rechabites and punishment to the house of Judah (Jer 35:12-19). Likewise, while in captivity in

No Wine-Drinking

Babylon, the prophet Daniel and his companions refuse to drink the wine that is offered to them (Dan 1:5, 8, 16; 10:3). Preserved in the Book of Proverbs is a queen mother's words to her son about it not being good for kings to drink wine (Prov 31:4). And in his Letter to the Romans, Paul makes clear that it is good not to drink wine if so doing would cause a brother or sister to stumble (Rom 14:21).

Meditation/Journal: When have you had the occasion to place limits on your personal liberty for the sake of others? Explain.

Prayer: Out of fidelity to you, O LORD, the Rechabites did not drink wine. Grant me the grace to know when to curb my personal liberty for the common good. Hear me through Christ my Lord. Amen.

10

Offering

Drink Offering 1

Scripture: Simon son of Onias "held out his hand for the cup and poured a drink offering of the blood of the grape; he poured it out at the foot of the altar, a pleasing odor to the Most High, the king of all." (Sir 50:15)

Reflection: Simon, a high priest, is described by the author of the OT (A) Book of Sirach as presenting a drink offering of red wine to God. According to the HB (OT) Book of Exodus, a drink offering of "one-fourth of a hin of wine" is to accompany the other animal sacrifices made during the consecration of Aaron and his sons as priests (Exod 29:40). A hin of wine is just a little over a gallon, so one-fourth of a hin is about a quart. The prophet Hosea records that Israel "shall not pour drink offerings of wine to the LORD" as punishment for idolatry (Hos 9:4a). The wine poured at the foot of the altar acknowledges that all blessings of the earth are from

Israel's God, the LORD, and that the Israelites are dependent upon him. When God decrees that the Israelites will no longer pour drink offerings of wine at the foot of the altar, he is effectively telling his people that because they have worship other gods, he will not accept their sacrifices. The equivalent of a drink offering today is the toast, a pronouncement of blessings, followed by the clinking of wine glasses to indicate that all form a communal connection to the kind words just spoken, and the drinking of a sip of wine.

Meditation/Journal: When have you most recently participated in a toast and clinked your wine glass with others before enjoying the wine? What were the wished-for blessings?

Prayer: Accept this prayer, heavenly Father, as a drink offering of the blood of the grape. May it be a pleasing odor to you, the Most High, the king of all now and forever. Amen.

Drink Offering 2

Scripture: " . . . [T]he LORD will vindicate his people, have compassion on his servants, when he sees that their power is gone, neither bond nor free remaining. Then he will say: Where are their gods, the rock in which they took refuge, who . . . drank the wine of their libations?" (Deut 32:36–38a)

Reflection: In Moses' song in the HB (OT) Book of Deuteronomy, the author refers to the LORD drinking the wine of the people's libations. A libation is the pouring of a liquid—here wine—as a sacrifice. Wine libations were usually poured at the foot of the altar so they could be consumed by the earth, created by God. In that way, the LORD drank the wine! The HB (OT) Book of Numbers records four kinds of offerings, each of which involves an amount of wine given as a drink offering. Accompanying a burnt offering of a lamb is one-fourth of a hin of wine (Num 15:5), about a gallon; accompanying a burnt offering of a ram is one-third of a hin of wine (Num 15:7), about a quart plus a pint and a half; accompanying a burnt offering of a bull is one half of a hin of wine (Num

15:10), about two quarts; and on the first day of every month the "drink offerings shall be half a hin of wine for a bull, one-third a hin for a ram, and one-fourth of a hin for a lamb" (Num 28:14a). By drinking the wine offering, the LORD and people become one, similar to those gathered around a table and sharing a bottle of wine.

Meditation/Journal: With whom have you most recently shared a glass of wine? What bonding occurred as a result of this?

Prayer: O LORD, you vindicate your people; you have compassion on your servants when you find them powerless. Accept my prayer this day as you used to accept the drink offerings of your people that my relationship with you may grow strong today and forever. Amen.

First Fruits

Scripture: "The LORD spoke to Moses: Speak to the people of Israel and say to them: When you enter the land that I am giving you and you reap its harvest, you shall bring . . . the first fruits of your harvest to the priest. . . . [T]he drink offering . . . shall be of wine, one-fourth of a hin." (Lev 23:9, 13)

Reflection: According to the HB (OT) Book of Leviticus, in the spring the first fruits, the first agricultural produce, which includes about a quart of wine, are brought to the priest, who raises them to the LORD; this act indicates God's acceptance of the wine, which is given to the religious leaders and their families for their sustenance. The Book of Deuteronomy also emphasizes that the first fruits of the wine be given to the levitical priests (Deut 18:4), and the Book of Nehemiah does the same (Neh 10:37, 39). The offering of the first fruit of the vine, that is, the wine, serves two purposes. The first is that it demonstrates one's dependence upon God for everything. The second is that it provides wine for the priests, who have no other means of support. Today, when a person uncorks a bottle of wine, he or she demonstrates dependence upon the vineyard owner for planting vines, dressing them, harvesting grapes, and processing grapes into wine. The individual also comes to realize that those often-migrant workers who work in the vineyard are dependent upon the consumer for their livelihood.

Meditation/Journal: Who are you supporting when you purchase a bottle of wine? Make a list of those involved in the vineyard, in the winery, and in the store where you purchased the bottle of wine.

Prayer: O LORD, you spoke to Moses and instructed him to tell the people of Israel to bring the first fruits of their harvest, including wine, to the priest. Accept my prayer of thanksgiving for the fruit of the vine and wine which is made from it. Amen.

Support of Ministers

Scripture: "I [, Tobit,] would hurry off to Jerusalem with the first fruits.... I would give these to the priests, the sons of Aaron, at the altar; likewise the tenth of the ... wine ..., and the rest of the fruits to the sons of Levi who ministered at Jerusalem." (Tobit 1:6b–7a)

Reflection: Tobit, in the OT (A) book of the same name, refers to the tenth of the wine given as first fruits to the priests and Levites as support for the temple ministers. The OT (A) Book of Judith also refers to the "tithes of the wine ..., which [the Israelites] had consecrated and set aside for the priests who minister in the presence of ... God in Jerusalem" (Jdt 11:13; cf. Ezra 6:9). This act flows from the LORD's words to Aaron in the HB (OT) Book of Numbers: "I have given to you, ... as a perpetual due, whatever is set aside from the gifts of all the elevation offerings of the Israelites.... [A]ll the best of the wine ... that they give to the LORD, I have given to you" (Num 18:11–12). The Book of Numbers also stipulates that from what the Levites receive, they are to tithe "the fullness of the wine press" (Num 18:27) or "the produce of the wine press" (Num 18:30) so that one tenth of the wine is given to the priests. The temple ministers are supported by the tithes of wine, among other tithes, because they have no other means of support. While most ministers are not supported by tithes of wine today, they rely upon the members of their congregations to support them with monetary offerings or tithes.

Meditation/Journal: If you belong to a church, how do you support its ministers? If you do not belong to a church, how do you support the work of charitable institutions in your area?

Prayer: You have instructed me, O LORD, to support those who minister in churches and in charitable works. Remove whatever selfishness keeps me from sharing your blessings with others. All praise to your boundless graciousness now and forever. Amen.

11

Metaphor for Life

Wine Is Life

Scripture: "Wine is very life to human beings if taken in moderation. What is life to one who is without wine? It has been created to make people happy. Wine drunk at the proper time and in moderation is rejoicing of heart and gladness of soul. Wine drunk to excess leads to bitterness of spirit, to quarrels and stumbling." (Sir 31:27–29)

Reflection: The wisdom of the OT (A) Book of Sirach presents a reflection on wine. Holding up a glass of wine, the author sees the whole of life. He advocates moderation or reasonableness in all things. Wine supports life as long as it is not drunk in excess. In fact, something is missing in life without wine! It makes people happy; it provides those who drink it with enjoyment, rejoicing their hearts or their whole physical being and giving gladness to their souls, their spiritual being. But when wine is consumed to excess, it results in bitterness to one's physical and spiritual being. Bitterness expresses itself in quarrels and stumbling. By pouring a glass of wine and looking upon it reflectively, a person can remember all the joy that has existed in his or her life. Likewise, by pouring a glass of wine and looking up at reflectively, a person can remember all the sorrow that has existed in his or her life. Joy and sorrow exist in everyone's life, just like they do in a glass of wine. The key is to keep them both in moderation.

Meditation/Journal: What joys and sorrows in your life does a glass of wine reveal to you?

Prayer: Ever-living God, wine is very life to the human beings you have created. It makes them happy, rejoicing their hearts and gladdening their souls. Grant me the gift of moderation in all things that I may not fall into excess bitterness of spirit. Amen.

Wine Is a Banquet

Scripture: "A ruby seal in a setting of gold is a concert of music at a banquet of wine. A seal of emerald in a rich setting of gold is the melody of music with good wine" (Sir 32:5–6).

Reflection: The OT (A) Book of Sirach refers to a banquet of wine several times (31:31; 49:1) including the one mentioned above. The author is referring to a feast at which wine is served and eating and drinking are accompanied by music. He says the beauty of a precious red stone named ruby in a gold setting is like the music played while red wine is served during a banquet. Likewise, the beauty of a precious green stone named emerald in a gold setting is like the music played while good wine is served during a feast. While modern people would not use the same comparisons, Sirach's point is well made. There is a difference between eating and dining. Eating refers to filling one's stomach with fast food. Dining refers to enjoying every bite of food while also engaging in conversation with those around one. One does not usually serve wine with fast food, but it is most likely present when a few people are dining.

Meditation/Journal: How do you distinguish eating from dining? When have you participated in a banquet of wine?

Prayer: There is nothing like wine and good music, LORD God, to make dining in your presence an enjoyable experience. Grant that I may one day share the eternal banquet in your kingdom, where you live and reign forever and ever. Amen.

Wine Is Love

Scripture: "Let him kiss me with the kisses of his mouth! For your love is better than wine." (Song 1:2)

Reflection: The HB (OT) Song of Songs or Song of Solomon begins with the unnamed woman stating that love is better than wine. She extols her unnamed lover more than wine (Song 1:4). Later, the unnamed man tells the woman, "How sweet is your love . . . ! How much better is your love than wine . . . " (Song 4:10). He adds, " . . . [Y]our kisses [are] like the best wine that goes down smoothly, gliding over lips and teeth" (Song 7:9). He compares her navel to "a rounded bowl that never lacks mixed wine" (Song 7:2) and her breasts to "clusters of the vine" (Song 7:8b). Their love is like the vines in blossom (Song 2:13; 6:11b). She invites him to "go out early to the vineyards, and see whether the vines have budded, whether the grape blossoms have opened" (Song 7:12). She desires to give him "spiced wine to drink" (Song 8:2b). The OT (A) Book of Sirach states that "wine tests hearts" (Sir 31:26). Authentic, honest, transparent love is like wine and better than wine. Like the blossoming of the vines, love blossoms over time and grows, producing fruit, producing a bouquet-filled, full bodied, clear wine between two people.

Meditation/Journal: How are love and wine connected in your life?

Prayer: Creator God, your love for people is better than wine. Grant that my love for you, like wine, will continue to grow all the days of my life. And grant that I may love others authentically, honestly, and transparently, like wine, in the hope of loving you and them for all eternity. Amen.

Wine Is a Woman

Scripture: "Happy is everyone who fears the LORD, who walks in his ways. Your wife will be like a fruitful vine within your house." (Ps 128:1, 3a)

Reflection: The psalmist declares happy those men who trust and obey God. Their wives will bear children like a grape vine bears fruit! While the image is not all that appealing today, in its own time—when a man's number of children determined his honor and future—the fruitful vine metaphor was a worthy designation for his wife. Thus, there are Sirach's words of advice: "Never dine with another man's wife, or revel with her at wine" (Sir 9:9a); "Wine and women lead intelligent men astray" (Sir 19:2). Again, these proverbs must be placed into their original cultural setting of the importance of a man's wife, whom he bought from her father, and her primary roles of bearing children and raising them. According to Sirach, a man should not share a meal with another man's wife because she belongs to another man, and he would look like he was attempting to seduce her. The combination of wine and women could easily lead astray an otherwise reasonable family man. Thus, the best course of action, according to Sirach, is for a man with a family to remain faithful to his own wife. Such wisdom should not be passed over lightly today.

Meditation/Journal: Granted the patriarchal cultural context of Sirach's sayings, what wine metaphor could be used appropriately in your culture today?

Prayer: Happy are those who trust you, O LORD! Happy are those who walk in your ways. You make them like fruitful vines within your house. Grant me fullness of days in your presence now and forever. Amen.

Wine Is a Friend

Scripture: "Do not abandon old friends, for new ones cannot equal them. A new friend is like new wine; when it has aged, you can drink it with pleasure." (Sir 9:10)

Reflection: A friend is a person who has a close, personal relationship of mutual affection and trust with another person. The author of the OT (A) Book of Sirach declares that one should not abandon old friends, because the time put into those relationships and the love and faith developed as a result of it cannot equal the beginning of a new friendship. Earlier, the author of Sirach had stated that a faithful friend is a sturdy shelter (Sir 6:13), beyond price (Sir 6:15), and a life-saving medicine (Sir 6:16). In other words, friendship is a treasure which cannot be counted; a good friend is a gift from God. An old friend is also like aged wine: full of flavor, bouquet, and body. A new friend is like new wine with little flavor, little bouquet, and thin. One spends quality time with an old friend, and it brings pleasure, just like drinking aged wine is pleasurable. One spends quality time with a new friend, and it, too, brings pleasure, but it is the pleasure of a developing relationship, just like newly fermented, but not yet aged, wine.

Meditation/Journal: Which of your friends is like aged wine? Explain how. Which of your friends is like new wine? Explain how.

Prayer: One of your many gifts, heavenly Father, is a friend. Hear this prayer for all my friends, both those who are aged and those who are new. May they find pleasure in me and I in them in the same way as I find it in a glass of wine. All praise be to you forever and ever. Amen.

12

Metaphor for Abundance

Full Yield

Scripture: The LORD let the hungry "plant vineyards and get a fruitful yield." (Ps 107:37)

Reflection: In the Bible, wine is used as a metaphor for abundance. Lengthy Psalm 107 gives thanks to God for a variety of things, including the fruitful yield of a vineyard. The prophet Joel writes about the restoration of the land after a plague of locusts declaring that the vine will give its full yield (Joel 2:22). Likewise, the prophet Zechariah promises restoration to the Jews stating that "the vine shall yield its fruit" (Zech 8:12). A fruitful yield or a full yield means that the vine is producing grapes at maximum capacity. An abundance of grapes are growing, and from those grapes an abundance of wine can be made. Such a promise was hardly a reality in the ancient world which lacked modern means of fertilizers to spur growth and sprays to protect the harvest from pests. The hope of abundance was just that, a hope. It required trust that

Metaphor for Abundance

God would provide for his people in their need. It is hard to engender such trust in modern people because many of them live in the midst of abundance.

Meditation/Journal: How does living in abundance get in your way of placing all your trust in God to provide?

Prayer: I give thanks to you, O LORD, for you are good; your steadfast love endures forever. Grant me a deeper trust in your providence that I may enjoy the abundance of your grace now and forever. Amen.

Wealth

Scripture: Jacob said: "Binding his foal to the vine and his donkey's colt to the choice vine, [Judah] washes his garments in wine and his robe in the blood of grapes; his eyes are darker than wine. . . . (Gen 49:11–12)

Reflection: In Jacob's final speech in the HB (OT) Book of Genesis, he praises the wealth of the tribe of Judah; since this text was composed after David and his successors, it is not difficult to see why the author mentions Judah's wealth. The demonstration of that wealth will be his ability to tie his donkey to the wealth of vines in the vineyard. He will enjoy so much prosperity that he will wash both his outer and under clothes in wine. Judah will drink so much wine that his eyes will be darker than wine. Such wealth is also expressed by Moses about Judah in the HB (OT) Book of Deuteronomy: " . . . Israel lives in safety; untroubled is Jacob's abode in a land of . . . wine, where the heavens drop down dew" (Deut 33:28). Jeremiah records that the remnant of the Jews left in Jerusalem, after the king of Babylon had attacked, gathered wine in great abundance (Jer 40:12), and Ezekiel mentions that Judah possessed an abundance of wine (Ezek 27:18). Even the OT (A) Book of Wisdom refers to costly wine (Wis 2:7). Thus, wealth can be calculated in terms of the wine one owns.

Meditation/Journal: What do you use to calculate your wealth? Make a list and estimate the value of the items on the list—such as house, car, boat, etc.—in order to calculate your wealth.

Prayer: Gracious God, it is out of your generosity that I am able to share in the wealth of the earth. Grant me an awareness of your many gifts, and give me a deeper appreciation for them. I raise a glass of wine to you in praise now and forever. Amen.

Blessing

Scripture: "Provide liberally out of . . . your wine press, thus giving . . . some of the bounty with which the LORD your God has blessed you." (Deut 15:14)

Reflection: The above verse from the HB (OT) Book of Deuteronomy is part of an instruction given to one who frees a slave after six years of slavery. When a person is set free, the former owner is instructed to share with the freed slave some of the blessings that God has shared with him. Repeatedly, the Book of Deuteronomy states that the LORD will bless the Israelites' wine if they remain faithful to his covenant (Deut 7:13, 11:14). In the Book of Genesis, when Isaac blesses Jacob, he prays that God will give him plenty of wine (Gen 27:28, 37). Isaiah, too, considers wine a blessing (Isa 65:8), as does Joel (2:19) and Hosea (2:8–9). A blessing is an acknowledgement that God has bestowed an unearned and undeserved gift out of pure generosity. A glass of wine can remind the person holding it of all the blessings he or she has received undeservedly. Just taking one day and making a list of one's blessings that day would be enough to prove this point.

Meditation/Journal: What blessings have you undeservedly received in the past couple of days? Make a list and use it in a prayer of thanksgiving.

Prayer: You provide liberally for my needs, O LORD, showering your bounteous blessings upon me. Thank you for these many gifts (mention the list you made from the meditation/journal exercise above). Please accept this prayer of thanks for these recognized blessings and those I have not yet recognized. Amen.

Future Blessings

Scripture: "I will restore the fortunes of my people Israel, and they shall rebuild the ruined cities and inhabit them; they shall plant vineyards and drink their wine, and they shall make gardens and eat their fruit," says the LORD. (Amos 9:14)

Reflection: God often speaks about future blessings for his people using the metaphors of a vineyard and wine, as noted above by the prophet Amos. The prophet Hosea also employs these metaphors portraying the LORD saying, " . . . I will now allure her, and bring her into the wilderness, and speak tenderly to her. From there I will give her her vineyards . . . " (Hos 2:14–15a). While Amos notes the rebuilding of cities with the replanting of vineyards, Hosea prefers the image of returning to the desert for formation before planting vineyards. All three of the major prophets use the vineyard metaphor to express future blessings for the Jews (Isa 37:30, 65:21; Jer 31:5, 32:15; Ezek 28:26). Thus, planting a vineyard is a sign of stability; one is going to be around for a while to take care of it. A vineyard represents permanence or settledness. Only people who live in houses or in cities plant and tend vineyards; nomads do not plant vineyards. A direct future blessing to planting a vineyard is drinking the wine made from the grapes that grow in it.

Meditation/Journal: What future blessings do you anticipate receiving from God?

Prayer: You promise to restore all those who trust in you, LORD God. Lift me up in your service and grant that I may enjoy your blessings in all my days to come. In your mercy, hear this prayer. Amen.

Not Gathering All Grapes

Scripture: "You shall not strip your vineyard bare, or gather the fallen grapes of your vineyard; you shall leave them for the poor and the alien: I am the LORD your God." (Lev 19:10)

Reflection: The HB (OT) Book of Leviticus makes it clear that the produce of the vine is not to be collected totally. Some grapes are to be left on the vine along with the grapes that fall off the clusters for the poor and the alien. In other words, owners of vineyards do not enjoy an absolute ownership of what their vineyards produce. The same law is found in the HB (OT) Book of Deuteronomy: "When you gather the grapes of your vineyard, do not glean what is left; it shall be for the alien, the orphan, and the widow" (Deut 24:21). This latter law expands the list of those who are entitled to the leftover grapes in the vineyard. The vineyard itself was protected from unfair exploitation by the poor: "If you go into your neighbor's vineyard, you may eat your fill of grapes, as many as you wish, but you shall not put any in a container" (Deut 23:24). Even the land upon which the vineyard is planted is protected from exploitation. The Book of Leviticus legislates that every seventh year the land will rest. Vineyards are not to be pruned, and the grapes that grow on the unpruned vine are not to be gathered (Lev 25:4–5). The same holds true for every fiftieth year (Lev 25:11). God owns all, and he protects all he created.

Meditation/Journal: How does knowing that no one has an absolute ownership of anything affect your presupposition of title to land, house, car, etc.? How does the concept of stewardship fit into your understanding?

Prayer: Creator God, since you made all that exists, I can lay claim to nothing in your world. Grant me a greater concern for the poor, the orphan, the widow, and the alien. Give me a spirit of stewardship in your service now and forever. Amen.

13

Metaphor for Poverty

Lack of Wealth

Scripture: "Whoever loves pleasure will suffer want; whoever loves wine . . . will not be rich." (Prov 21:17)

Reflection: If wine can be used as a metaphor for abundance, the lack of it can also be used as a metaphor for poverty. The HB (OT) Book of Proverbs expresses that thought. Those who love wine spend their money on it; therefore, they will not be rich. Their monetary resources will be spent on the pleasure they love, and they will suffer want. Isaiah, even though he has just declared that the LORD is going to lay waste the earth, softens Proverbs' words: "No longer do they drink wine with singing; strong drink is bitter to those who drink it. There is an outcry in the streets for lack of wine; all joy has reached its eventide; the gladness of the earth is banished" (Isa 24:9, 11). Isaiah's poetry expresses a poverty of wine-drinking, singing, joy, and gladness because there is no wine.

The prophet considers wine-drinking, singing, joy, and gladness to be among one's wealth. Spending all one's money on wine, however, leaves none for the basic human necessities of food, clothing, and housing, and plunges the person into penury. Thus, the lack of wine is a fitting metaphor for poverty.

Meditation/Journal: What want do you suffer? What is the cause of your suffering?

Prayer: Whoever loves pleasure more than you, O LORD, suffers want; whoever loves wine more than you, O LORD, will never be rich. Grant me a greater love for you, and make me rich in good works. Amen.

Destroyed

Scripture: "On that day every place where there used to be a thousand vines, worth a thousand shekels of silver, will become briers and thorns." (Isa 7:23)

Reflection: Poverty is the result of the destruction of a vineyard. The prophet Isaiah uses the image of briers and thorns to speak about the destruction of the land by soldiers with bows and arrows (Isa 7:24). Lengthy Psalm 78 explains how the LORD destroyed the vines of the Egyptians with hail (Ps 78:47) while Psalm 105 states that he struck their vines with lightning (Ps 105:33). The prophet Zephaniah lists one of the punishments that God intents to inflict upon his people as not being able to drink the wine from their vineyards (Zeph 1:13). Not only do modern people not like thinking or talking about destruction, but they also do not like reading about it in the Bible. The poverty that results from destroyed vineyards reminds wealthy people, just like it reminded wealthy biblical folks, that some things need to be destroyed in order to begin again. While a destroyed vineyard is a metaphor for poverty, a restored one is a metaphor for wealth.

Metaphor for Poverty

Meditation/Journal: What event in your life left you with destruction? How was it restored?

Prayer: You, O LORD, bring into existence, and you destroy what you have created. Help me to understand the wisdom of your ways that I might welcome the destruction that leads to new life in my life now and forever. Amen.

Withered

Scripture: " . . . [T]he wine dries up. . . . The vine withers. . . . " (Joel 1:10b, 12a)

Reflection: Another metaphor for poverty is the dried up wine and the withered vine. For the prophet Joel the dried up wine and the withered vine were the result of a locust plague. However, both dried up wine and withered vines could be the result of no grapes. In his speech to Job, Eliphaz states that the wicked "shake off their unripe grape, like the vine" (Job 15:33a). The prophet Jeremiah records the LORD saying, "When I wanted to gather [the people], . . . there are no grapes on the vine, . . . even the leaves are withered . . . " (Jer 8:13). For Jeremiah, Israel the vine did not keep her covenant with the LORD; she withered into idolatry. Some liquids, when kept for a long period of time, dry up, becoming merely sticky dregs in the bottom of a bottle. Some plants, when given too much water or not enough, dry up, becoming merely sticks and twigs. Such dried up and withered imagery is easily applied to people who have stopped growing, exercising, reading, learning, etc. In some way they are like the living dead. A dried up bottle of wine or a withered vine serves as a reminder never to stop improving oneself.

Meditation/Journal: What event in your life was like dried up wine or a withered vine? How did you get new life from it?

Prayer: Heavenly Father, pour on me the grace of the Holy Spirit that I may never cease to grow in your presence. When you come looking for grapes on my vine, grant that I may provide you with an abundance in this life that make new wine in the life to come. Amen.

Sour Grapes

Scripture: "... [J]ust as I have watched over [the house of Israel] to pluck up and break down, to overthrow, destroy, and bring evil, so I will watch over them to build and to plant, says the LORD. In those days they shall no longer say: 'The parents have eaten sour grapes, and the children's teeth are set on edge.'" (Jer 31:28–29)

Reflection: The proverb about parents eating sour grapes and children's teeth set on edge recorded by Jeremiah is also recorded by Ezekiel: "The word of the LORD came to me: What do you mean by repeating this proverb concerning the land of Israel, 'The parents have eaten sour grapes, and the children's teeth are set on edge?'" (Ezek 18:1–2) The proverb means that a previous generation (parents) sinned, but the current generation is paying the consequences for it. It is an accusation that God is unjust. Instead of taking responsibility for their actions, people were blaming their ancestors. Both Jeremiah and Ezekiel attack the proverb, declaring that every person bears responsibility for his or her behavior and, consequently, for his or her good deeds or sin. Thus, eating sour grapes is an appropriate metaphor for poverty. Not only does one not like sour grapes, but they become a poor means of not taking responsibility for one's behavior. This generation is as responsible for its (in)action as the previous one.

Meditation/Journal: Whom have you blamed recently for your current state of affairs? In other words, who ate sour grapes and set your teeth on edge?

Prayer: Just as you watch over your people to pluck up and to break down, to overthrow, destroy, and bring evil, so you watch over them to build and to plant, O LORD. Give me the strength to take responsibility for my deeds, as you guide me in the paths of righteousness all the days of my life. Amen.

Devoured

Scripture: "The LORD enters into judgment with the elders and princes of his people: It is you who have devoured the vineyard; the spoil of the poor is in your houses." (Isa 3:14)

Reflection: The prophet Isaiah declares that God judges the ruling groups of the Israelites, and he discovers that they have consumed the vineyard, that is, they have gleaned everything and left nothing for the poor. What was due the poor, according to God's Torah—the leftover grapes and the grapes fallen on the ground—has been harvested by the elders and princes. The spoil of the poor is in their homes. The poor have been oppressed, plundered, and what was due to them has been taken violently. The LORD is both judge and accuser bringing the rulers to trial and finding them guilty for having devoured the vineyard. Devoured is another good metaphor for poverty. Those who devour what belongs to the poor leave the poor poorer. This is seen around the world as big corporations, focused only on unbridled wealth, leave the poor workers and move to another place for cheaper labor where more poor are left poorer. God declares this to be unjust; it violates the rights of his favorite people: the poor.

Meditation/Journal: Who has devoured the vineyard in your part of the world? What poor were left behind?

Prayer: O LORD, just judge, you condemn the rulers of the world who devour your resources, leaving nothing for the poor. Never let me forget those special people to whom you have promised care, and grant me the wisdom to use my resources to alleviate some of their poverty. Amen.

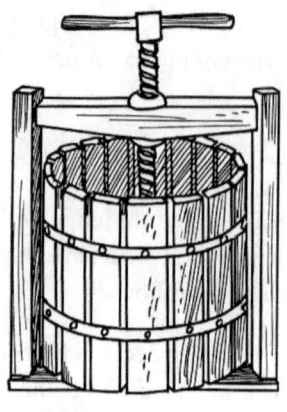

14

Metaphor for Wrath

Wine Press 1

Scripture: "'Why are your robes red, and your garments like theirs who tread the wine press?' 'I have trodden the wine press alone, and from the peoples no one was with me; I trod them in my anger and trampled them in my wrath; their juice spattered on my garments, and stained all my robes.'" (Isa 63:2–3)

Reflection: Because a wine press was a method of pressing or squeezing grapes until only the skin and seeds remained, it easily became a metaphor for God's wrath. Jeremiah describes the LORD roaring from on high against his people and shouting "like those who tread grapes" (Jer 25:30). The HB (OT) Book of Lamentations declares that "the Lord has trodden as in a wine press the virgin daughter Judah" (Lam 1:15). The prophet Joel extends the wrath metaphor to the harvest and applies it to Israel's enemies, writing, "Put in the sickle, for the harvest is ripe. Go in, tread, for the wine press is full. The vats overflow, for their wickedness is great" (Joel 3:13). God's anger and wrath are like a wine press that crushes infidelity and wickedness by squeezing the life out of them! The experience of God's anger and wrath is like feeling pressed; it is like being caught between a rock and hard place. While the LORD tolerates some evil, there is a point in time, according to biblical authors, when he decides to destroy it.

Meditation/Journal: Have you ever experienced someone's anger as being like a wine press? Explain.

Prayer: Your righteous wrath, LORD God, is like those treading the wine press. Spare me your anger and wrath by forgiving my wickedness. I praise you for your mercy now and forever. Amen.

Wine Press 2

Scripture: "So the angel swung his sickle over the earth and gathered the vintage of the earth, and he threw it into the great wine press of the wrath of God. And the wine press was trodden outside the city, and blood flowed from the wine press, as high as a horse's bridle, for a distance of about two hundred miles." (Rev 14:19–20)

Reflection: No biblical author loves the image of the wine press as a metaphor for God's wrath more than John of Patmos, the pseudonymous author of the CB (NT) Book of Revelation. He condemns Babylon (Rome) for having made all the nations drink of the wine of the wrath of her fornication (Rev 14:8; 18:3); she gets "the wine-cup of the fury of [God's] wrath" (Rev 16:19). He declares that those who worship the beast (evil empires) will "drink the wine of God's wrath, poured unmixed into the cup of his anger" (Rev 14:10). The heavenly warrior "will tread the wine press of the fury of the wrath of God the Almighty" (Rev 19:15). These violent images predicated of God give the reader pause. This climatic and final destruction of evil, meant to scare people into changing their behaviors, turns God into a violent despot— which image is all but ignored today. Trampling, destruction, and judgment are not usually associated with the God who is also said to be rich in mercy.

Meditation/Journal: What feelings about God does the imagery from the Book of Revelation evoke in you? How do you balance those feelings with those associated with God's mercy?

Prayer: Father, the end of the world is imaged as the gathering of the vintage of the earth and it being thrown into the great wine press of your wrath. Guide my steps that I not be placed into that wine press but admitted to your presence where I will praise you forever and ever. Amen.

Cup of Wrath

Scripture: " . . . [I]n the hand of the LORD there is a cup with foaming wine, well mixed; he will pour a draught from it, and all the wicked of the earth shall drain it down to the dregs." (Ps 75:8)

Reflection: In Psalm 75, the wrath of God is compared to drinking a cup of wine and draining it down to the dregs. A person experiencing God's wrath drinks wholly of it in order to suffer its consequences. The Book of Proverbs refers to this as drinking the wine of violence (Prov 4:17). In the Book of Jeremiah, God commands the prophet to act as a wine steward to the kings of major nations around Judah, saying, "Take from my hand this cup of the wine of wrath, and make all the nations to whom I send you drink it" (Jer 25:15). According to this metaphor, God intends punishment, and he makes those he intends to punish drink from the cup of wrath. Jeremiah records that he did as the LORD directed him, making all the nations to whom the LORD sent him drink it; they became a desolation and a waste, objects of hissing and of cursing (Jer 25:17–18). In a long narrative (Jer 25:16–38), Jeremiah describes all those who drank from the cup. God directs the prophet to say, "Drink, get drunk, and vomit, fall and rise no more . . . " (Jer 25:27); in other words, God intends punishment. Like the image of the wine press, the image of drinking the cup of God's wrath does not sit well with modern people.

Meditation/Journal: What bothers you most about the metaphor of drinking the wine cup of God's wrath? Explain.

Prayer: In your hand, O LORD, there is a cup with foaming wine, well mixed, from which you will pour a draught, and all the wicked of the earth shall drain it down to the dregs. May your grace preserve me from sharing that cup. Surround me with your everlasting mercy now and forever. Amen.

No Wine-Drinking

Scripture: Moses said to the people, "You shall plant vineyards and dress them, but you shall neither drink the wine nor gather the grapes, for the worm shall eat them." (Deut 28:39)

Reflection: Among the metaphors for God's wrath is one of the curses for disobedience found in the HB (OT) Book of Deuteronomy. According to the curse, the vineyard will produce no grapes and no wine. The grapes will be infested with worms, and they cannot be used to make wine. The prophet Amos levies this curse on those who trample the poor; they may plant pleasant vineyards, but they will not drink wine from them (Amos 5:11). Likewise, the prophet Zephaniah declares that on the day of the LORD those who rest complacently on their dregs will have their wealth plundered; "though they plant vineyards, they shall not drink wine from them" (Zeph1:13c). Those who are undisturbed, as is the sediment of wine, will be punished by God; their punishment will be no wine. While that may not sound like punishment to modern people, to folks who dared not drink the water, this is punishment that has a double effect: no wine to drink and only contaminated water to drink which results in illness. Thus, while having no wine to drink is less violent than the image of the wine press and cup, it, nevertheless, serves as a metaphor for God's wrath.

Meditation/Journal: Why do you think the metaphor of having no wine to drink to describe God's wrath is appropriate or not appropriate today? Explain.

Prayer: You curse those who disobey you, O LORD, and you curse those who ignore the poor in their midst. With your grace going before and after me do not let me become hard of heart. Give me the willingness to serve you by serving those in need that I may hope to share in your eternal blessings now and forever. Amen.

15

Metaphor for Blood

Blood of the Grape

Scripture: "The basic necessities of human life are water and fire ..., and ... the blood of the grape...." (Sir 39:26)

Reflection: Among a list of the basic necessities to preserve human life the author of the OT (A) Book of Sirach lists the blood of the grape. The author also describes a high priest pouring a drink offering of the blood of the grape (Sir 50:15). Because most wine made in the ancient world was red, and red is the color of oxygenated blood, wine was often referred to as the blood of the grape. The patriarch Jacob's last words declare that his son Judah will wash his clothes in the blood of grapes (Gen 49:11b). The HB (OT) Book of Deuteronomy mentions that Jacob, Israel, "drank fine wine from the blood of the grapes" (Deut 32:14). However, it is the prophet Isaiah who explicitly explains the metaphor when he describes Israel's oppressors as getting "drunk with their own blood as with wine" (Isa 49:26a). Modern sensibilities probably keep people from referring to red wine as the blood of the grape, because it would indicate that one is drinking blood, which would be repulsive.

Meditation/Journal: What connotations does the metaphor blood of the grape have for you?

Prayer: Almighty God, fine, red wine resembling blood is one of your many gifts to people. Grant me the enjoyment of this benevolence now and forever. Amen.

Blood of the (New) Covenant

Scripture: Jesus "took a cup, and after giving thanks he gave it to [his disciples], and all of them drank from it. He said to them, 'This is my blood of the covenant, which is poured out for many.'" (Mark 14:23–24)

Reflection: Even though he does not state that there is wine in the cup which Jesus takes, the author of Mark's Gospel presumes it. It is the blood of the grape in the cup that Jesus announces is his blood of the covenant. Matthew's version of this event follows Mark's narrative: Jesus takes a cup, presumably filled with wine because he and his disciples are celebrating Passover which requires the use of wine, gives thanks, and gives it to his disciples, instructing them to drink from it because it is his blood of the covenant poured out for many for the forgiveness of sins (Matt 26:27–28). The author of Luke's Gospel, who notes two of the cups of wine used at Passover, states that Jesus took the cup after supper, saying, "This cup that is poured out for you is the new covenant in my blood" (Luke 22:20). Paul asks the Corinthians, "The cup of blessing that we bless, is it not a sharing in the blood of Christ?" (1 Cor 10:16) Later, in the same letter Paul narrates how Jesus took the cup after supper, saying, "This cup is the new covenant in my blood" (1 Cor 11:25). In each of these biblical versions of the Lord's Supper, the wine in the cup is associated with the metaphor of the blood of the grape, and

Metaphor for Blood

that metaphor becomes Jesus' blood of the (new) covenant echoing the blood of the previous covenant (Exod 24:6–8).

Meditation/Journal: With what do you associate blood?

Prayer: While celebrating Passover, almighty Father, Jesus, your Son, took a cup of wine and named the blood of grapes his own blood. Grant that I may drink deeply of this life-giving wine. I ask this in name of Jesus Christ, who is Lord forever and ever. Amen.

Thanksgiving

Scripture: Jesus "took a cup, and after giving thanks he gave it to [his disciples], saying, 'Drink from it, all of you; for this is my blood of the covenant, which is poured out for many for the forgiveness of sins.'" (Matt 26:27–28)

Reflection: During the celebration of Passover at the time of Jesus, the leader took several cups of red wine, lifted them, and offered thanksgiving to God. Since wine was a gift from God, it was offered to him in thanksgiving. The accounts of the Lord's Supper in the CB (NT) mention that Jesus took the cup with the blood of grapes and gave thanks (Mark 14:23; Matt 26:27; Luke 22:17). Paul refers to it as the cup of blessing (1 Cor 10:16). The Eucharistic Prayers in *The Roman Missal* maintain this narrative of Jesus giving thanks and blessing.[1] Furthermore, after pouring wine into the cup, the priest or bishop lifts it slightly above the altar and says: "Blessed are you, Lord God of all creation, for through your goodness we have received the wine we offer you: fruit of the vine and work of human hands, it will become our spiritual drink."[2] The prayer, specifically drawn from the words of Passover, blesses or praises God for his goodness manifested as the wine, the fruit of the vine,

---

1. *Roman Missal*, "The Order of Mass," pars. 90, 103, 111, 120; "Appendix to the Order of Mass: Eucharistic Prayer for Reconciliation I," par. 5; "Eucharistic Prayer for Reconciliation II," par. 5; "Eucharistic Prayer for Various Needs I, II, III, IV," par. 5.

2. *Roman Missal*, "The Order of Mass," par. 25.

in the cup. Thus, the blood of the grape is offered in thanksgiving to God.

Meditation/Journal: When you pour and drink a glass of wine, do you ever think of offering thanksgiving to God for the blood of the grape? If so, what do you say or think? If not, why not?

Prayer: Creator God, because of your goodness I am able to pour and drink the fruit of the vine. Accept the blessing I offer you for the blood of the grape now and forever. Amen.

Drink Offering

Scripture: "Who knows whether he will not turn and relent, and leave a blessing behind him, . . . a drink offering for the LORD, your God?" (Joel 2:14)

Reflection: While the HB (OT) Book of Numbers contains over thirty references to drink offerings, it is the prophet Joel who suggests that repentance on the part of the people, as demonstrated with a drink offering, may result in blessings from the LORD. There is no doubt that the concept of the drink offering is present in *The Roman Missal*. After pouring wine into the chalice, the deacon or priest adds a little water, praying, "By the mystery of this water and wine may we come to share in the divinity of Christ who humbled himself to share in our humanity."[3] The meaning assigned to the ritual of mixing wine with a little water is that it represents the divinity and humanity of Jesus Christ. In its original context, the little bit of water was warmed and poured around the rim of the metal chalice in cold climates in order to keep one's lips from sticking to the cold metal! The ritual was not lost; it was merely adapted for heated buildings. After the water is poured into the wine, the mixture is offered to God[4]—it becomes a drink

---

3. Ibid., par. 24.
4. Ibid., par. 25.

Metaphor for Blood

offering—and is called a sacrifice.[5] After it is consecrated the blood of the grape will be consumed by those participating in the sacrificial drink offering.

Meditation/Journal: In what ways can your glass of wine be considered a drink offering to God?

Prayer: LORD God, you accepted drink offerings of wine from your people as a demonstration of their thanksgiving for the blessings you bestowed upon them. Make me aware of your countless gifts and accept the glass of wine I raise in blessing to you now and forever. Amen.

Fruit of the Vine

Scripture: Jesus "took a cup, and after giving thanks he said [to his disciples], 'Take this and divide it among yourselves; for I tell you that from now on I will not drink of the fruit of the vine until the kingdom of God comes.'" (Luke 22:17–18)

Reflection: As already noted, Jesus refers to the wine in the cup as the fruit of the vine in the gospels (Mark 14:25; Matt 26:29; Luke 22:18). "The General Instruction of the Roman Missal," found in *The Roman Missal*, states: "The wine for the celebration of the Eucharist must be from the fruit of the vine (cf. Lk 22:18), natural, and unadulterated, that is, without admixture of extraneous substances."[6] In the Eucharistic Prayers, the fruit of the vine is often referred to as the chalice,[7] the precious chalice,[8] or the chalice of blessing.[9] However, in Eucharistic Prayer IV, it is called "the chalice filled with the fruit of the vine"[10] as it is also referred

---

5. Ibid., pars. 26, 29.
6. *Roman Missal*, "General Instruction of the Roman Missal," par. 322.
7. Ibid., "The Order of Mass," pars. 103, 111; "Eucharistic Prayer for Various Needs I, II, III, IV," par. 5.
8. Ibid., "The Order of Mass," par. 90.
9. Ibid., "Eucharistic Prayer for Reconciliation II," par. 5.
10. Ibid., "The Order of Mass," par. 120.

to in Eucharistic Prayer for Reconciliation I.[11] Since the Mass is the new version of Passover, most of the Eucharistic Prayers presume that the fruit of the vine is in the chalice—what the gospels call the cup—but two of them actually name the wine as the fruit of the vine in the chalice, as does the prayer accompanying the offering of the chalice with the wine mixed with a little water.[12]

Meditation/Journal: Why do you think it is so important that wine must be from the fruit of the vine, natural, and unadulterated, that is, without admixture of extraneous substances?

Prayer: On the night before he died, heavenly Father, your Son, Jesus, took a cup filled with the fruit of the vine, and after giving thanks, he gave it to his disciples and indicated that he would not drink of the fruit of the vine until your kingdom comes. As I remember his last supper, grant that I may experience to some degree now the coming of your kingdom, where you live and reign as one God—Father, Son, and Holy Spirit—forever and ever. Amen.

---

11. Ibid., "Appendix to the Order of Mass: Eucharistic Prayer for Reconciliation I," par. 5.

12. Ibid., "The Order of Mass," par. 25.

Other Books by Mark G. Boyer

History of St. Joachim Parish: 1822—1972; 1723—1973
Day by Day through the Easter Season
Following the Star: Daily Reflections for Advent and Christmas
Mystagogy: Liturgical Paschal Spirituality for Lent and Easter
Return to the Lord: A Lenten Journey of Daily Reflections
The Liturgical Environment: What the Documents Say
Breathing Deeply of God's New Life: Preparing Spiritually for the Sacraments of Initiation
Mary's Day—Saturday: Meditations for Marian Celebrations
Why Suffer?: The Answer of Jesus
A Month-by-Month Guide to Entertaining Angels
Biblical Reflections on Male Spirituality
"Seeking Grace with Every Step": The Spirituality of John Denver
Home Is a Holy Place
Day by Ordinary Day with Mark
Day by Ordinary Day with Matthew
Day by Ordinary Day with Luke
Baptized into Christ's Death and Resurrection: Preparing to Celebrate a Christian Funeral: Vol. 1: Adults
Baptized into Christ's Death and Resurrection: Preparing to Celebrate a Christian Funeral: Vol. 2: Children
The Greatest Gift of All: Reflections and Prayers for the Christmas Season
Meditations for Ministers
Waiting in Joyful Hope: Reflections for Advent 2001
Filled with New Light: Reflections for Christmas 2001-2002
Lent and Easter Prayer at Home
Using Film to Teach New Testament
Waiting in Joyful Hope: Daily Reflections for Advent and Christmas 2002-2003
Waiting in Joyful Hope: Daily Reflections for Advent and Christmas 2003-2004

Other Books by Mark G. Boyer

The Liturgical Environment: What the Documents Say (second edition)
Reflections on the Rosary
When Day Is Done: Nighttime Prayers through the Church Year
Take Up Your Cross and Follow: Daily Lenten Reflections
These Thy Gifts: A Collection of Simple Meal Prayers
Day by Ordinary Day: Daily Reflections on the First Readings, Year One
Day by Ordinary Day: Daily Reflections on the First Readings, Year Two
Mountain Reflections: A Collection of Photos and Meditations
Nature Spirituality: Praying with Wind, Water, Earth, Fire
A Spirituality of Ageing
Caroling through Advent and Christmas: Daily Reflections with Familiar Hymns
Weekday Saints: Reflections on Their Scriptures
Human Wholeness: A Spirituality of Relationship
The Liturgical Environment: What the Documents Say (third edition)
A Simple Systematic Mariology
Praying Your Way through Luke's Gospel and the Acts of the Apostles
Daybreaks: Daily Reflections for Advent and Christmas
Daybreaks: Daily Reflections for Lent and Easter
An Abecedarian of Animal Spirit Guides: Spiritual Growth through Reflections on Creatures
Overcome with Paschal Joy: Chanting through Lent and Easter—Daily Reflections with Familiar Hymns
Taking Leave of Your Home: Moving in the Peace of Christ
An Abecedarian of Sacred Trees: Spiritual Growth through Reflections on Woody Plants
A Spirituality of Mission: Reflections for Holy Week and Easter
Divine Presence: Elements of Biblical Theophanies

Bibliography

"Appendix to the Order of Mass: Eucharistic Prayer for Reconciliation I." In *The Roman Missal*, 758–64. Collegeville, MN: Liturgical, 2011.
"Appendix to the Order of Mass: Eucharistic Prayer for Reconciliation II." In *The Roman Missal*, 766–71. Collegeville, MN: Liturgical, 2011.
"Appendix to the Order of Mass: Eucharistic Prayer for Various Needs I, II, III, IV." In *The Roman Missal*, 774–97. Collegeville, MN: Liturgical, 2011.
"General Instruction of the Roman Missal, The." In *The Roman Missal*, 17–87. Collegeville, MN: Liturgical, 2011.
McKenzie, John L. *Dictionary of the Bible*. Milwaukee: Bruce, 1965.
Meir, John P. *A Marginal Jew: Rethinking the Historical Jesus* 5. New Haven, CT: Yale University Press, 2016.
O'Day, Gail R., and David Peterson, eds. *The Access Bible: New Revised Standard Version with the Apocryphal/Deuterocanonical Books*. New York: Oxford University Press, 1999.
"Order of Mass, The." In *The Roman Missal*, 511–689. Collegeville, MN: Liturgical, 2011.
Roberts, J.J.M. *First Isaiah*. Hermeneia. Minneapolis: Fortress, 2015.
Roman Missal, The. Collegeville, MN: Liturgical, 2011.
Ryken, Leland, James C. Wilhoit, and Tremper Longman III, eds. *Dictionary of Biblical Imagery*. Downers Grove, IL: InterVarsity, 1998.
Shapiro, Rami. "Roadside Assistance for the Spiritual Traveler." *Spirituality & Health* 19:3 (2016) 19–20.

www.ingramcontent.com/pod-product-compliance
Lightning Source LLC
Chambersburg PA
CBHW070632220426
R18178600001B/R181786PG43193CBX00018B/25